M000189876

Journey through the New Testament

Journey through the New Testament

Understanding the Purpose,
Themes, and Practical Implications of
Each New Testament Book of the Bible

William F. Cook III

THOM S. RAINER, SERIES EDITOR

TYNDALE
MOMENTUM®

A Tyndale nonfiction imprint

Visit Tyndale online at tyndale.com.

Visit Tyndale Momentum online at tyndalemomentum.com.

Tyndale, Tyndale's quill logo, *Tyndale Momentum*, and the Tyndale Momentum logo are registered trademarks of Tyndale House Ministries. Tyndale Momentum is a nonfiction imprint of Tyndale House Publishers, Carol Stream, Illinois.

Journey through the New Testament: Understanding the Purpose, Themes, and Practical Implications of Each New Testament Book of the Bible

Designed by Ron C. Kaufmann

For information about special discounts for bulk purchases, please contact Tyndale House Publishers at csresponse@tyndale.com, or call 1-855-277-9400.

Library of Congress Cataloging-in-Publication Data

A catalog record for this book is available from the Library of Congress.

ISBN 978-1-4964-6192-6

Printed in the United States of America

28 27 26 25 24 23 22
7   6   5   4   3   2   1

Contents

Beginning Our Journey Together

GOD'S SPIRIT USES God's Word to conform God's people into the image of God's Son, Jesus Christ. Whether you are preparing for vocational Christian ministry or are just beginning your acquaintance with the Bible, this book is for you.

Although *Journey through the New Testament* introduces readers to the "second half" of the Bible, don't think of it as a traditional introduction. Many New Testament introductions provide comprehensive background information on each book, discussing details of authorship, date, and provenance. *Journey through the New Testament* focuses more on the content of each book and asks readers to use it with an open Bible. We live in a biblically illiterate culture, which means we must work hard to master the content and major themes of each New Testament book.

I am both a seminary professor and a pastor. I have taught ministerial students for more than thirty years and have served more than twenty years as lead pastor at the Ninth and O Baptist Church in Louisville, Kentucky. These dual roles have provided me the opportunity to train future servants of the church while implementing in the local church what I teach my seminary students. All ministerial training should glorify Christ and build up the church.

The church of Jesus Christ needs men and women saturated in biblical truth. Everything that ministers of the gospel do should begin with the Word of God. We regularly read today about the fall of once-influential Christian leaders who knew the Word of God intellectually, but who did not allow the Word of God to daily transform their lives. This is why I ask you to read this book with an open Bible. As you read, look up every Scripture passage and cross-reference. As you read *about* Matthew's Gospel, for example, also read the *text* of Matthew's Gospel. Measure my words by God's Word. I want to help you become better equipped to serve the church of Jesus Christ.

The church needs competent servants in the Word who have a passion for God and who also love the church. A calling to gospel ministry is wonderful but not easy. Satan, a roaring lion, seeks whom he may devour (1 Peter 5:8). John the apostle describes the church's archenemy as a dragon, making war against the saints (Revelation 12:17). God has not abandoned us to our foe, but rather indwells us by his Spirit, gives us access into his presence, and provides us with the sword of the Spirit, the Word of God (Ephesians 6:17). God is still looking for men and women ready to be used for Kingdom advancement.

PART I

The Gospels and Acts

THE FOUR GOSPELS and the book of Acts make up nearly 60 percent of the New Testament.[1] The Gospels focus on the life of Christ, while Acts recounts the expansion of the church. The word *gospel* means "good news." The four Gospels present the Good News concerning Jesus Christ. Each Gospel tells the story of Jesus from the author's own perspective. The four Gospels resemble each other at certain points, while at other points look quite distinct.

The Gospels of Matthew, Mark, and Luke—known as the synoptic Gospels—resemble each other much more than John's Gospel. In fact, approximately 90 percent of John's Gospel is unique to him. The word *synoptic* means to look at something from a common perspective. Though the first three Gospels have much in common, they still present Jesus' life from their own distinctive vantage points. For Matthew, Jesus is the long-awaited

Jewish Messiah, the Son of David. For Mark, Jesus is the powerful, miracle-working Son of God. Luke presents Jesus as the Savior of all people. John, writing last, declares that Jesus Christ is God. As you read the Gospels, pray that the Holy Spirit will develop in you a greater love for Jesus and a greater passion to take his message across the street and around the world.

The book of Acts picks up where the Gospels leave off, especially Luke's Gospel. Luke, a traveling companion of Paul, wrote both the third Gospel and Acts. Acts traces the spread of the Good News from Jerusalem to Rome. Along the way, Luke tells stories to help his readers trust God to do great things through them.

Matthew

Jesus Is the Son of David

THE GOSPEL OF MATTHEW serves as a doorway from the Old Testament into the New Testament. If the author is the apostle Matthew (Levi), it could not have been written by a more unlikely candidate. Before Matthew followed Jesus, he worked as a tax collector (Matthew 9:9). His fellow Jews would have hated him because of his collaboration with Rome.

But the question remains: Did Matthew write the first Gospel? Strictly speaking, the writer is anonymous, unless the superscription ("According to Matthew") was part of the Gospel from its beginning. More likely, scribes added the superscription around AD 125 to distinguish it from the other Gospels. Whether the superscription formed an original part of the Gospel or was added early in the second century, it provides strong evidence for Matthew's authorship. In addition, the early church writers unanimously affirmed Matthew as the author of the Gospel. It is hard to imagine the early church attributing the Gospel to a former tax collector—one of the lesser-known apostles—unless he wrote it.

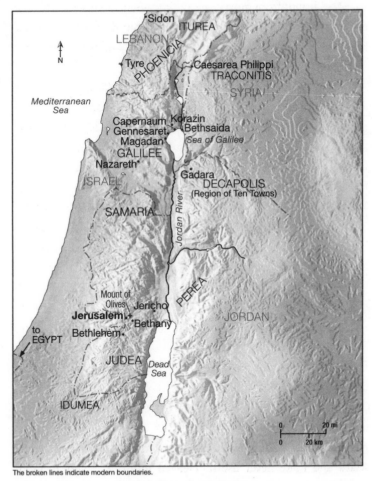

The broken lines indicate modern boundaries.

Key Places in Matthew

The Big Picture

What do we know about Matthew? Not much, but we can gain some insights about him from reading his Gospel. Since the Jewish people despised tax collectors and typically thought of them as traitors because of their collaboration with Rome, Matthew would have felt distant from most of his countrymen and disenfranchised by the Jewish religion. Matthew's authorship demonstrates Jesus' power to change the lives of the most unlikely of people, even tax collectors.

Who was the target audience for Matthew's Gospel? It appears the author intended it for Jewish-Christian readers. Matthew quotes the Old Testament approximately fifty times, with another seventy or so allusions to it. Matthew's "fulfillment formula," where he specifically indicates that certain events happened "to fulfill" biblical prophecies, suggests a Jewish audience (Matthew 1:22-23; 2:15; 2:17-18; 2:23; 4:14-16; 8:17; 12:17-21; 13:35; 21:4-5; 27:9-10).[2] We also see this Jewish-Christian perspective in the Gospel's emphasis on Jesus as the "Son [descendant] of David." Matthew uses the phrase eight times in referring to Jesus (Matthew 1:1; 9:27; 12:23; 15:22; 20:30-31; 21:9, 15; 22:41-45). Seven of these occurrences do not appear in the parallel material in Mark and Luke. Mark uses the title three times, and Luke uses it four. Oddly enough, those who recognize Jesus as the Son of David are consistently pictured as helpless or outcast (Matthew 9:27; 15:22; 20:30).

Matthew's use of "Kingdom of Heaven" instead of "Kingdom of God" provides another example of the Gospel's Jewishness. Matthew uses "Kingdom of Heaven" thirty-four times, while Mark and Luke never use it. Heaven indirectly refers to God, since Jewish people had an aversion to referring directly to the supremely holy God. The two phrases, however, are used more or less synonymously.

Though Matthew's Gospel is written from a Jewish-Christian perspective, it is intended ultimately for all Christians everywhere, which the Gospel makes clear in several ways. The first visitors mentioned by Matthew to worship the Christ child, for example, were Magi from the East (Matthew 2:1-12). In the parable of the wheat and the tares recorded in Matthew 13, the sower (Jesus) sows his seed (the sons of the righteous) in his field, which is the world. The Gospel concludes with Jesus' famous Great Commission to make disciples of all peoples (Matthew 28:16-20). Furthermore, at strategic places in the Gospel, Jesus ministers to Gentiles (Matthew 8:5-13; 15:21-28). The only two references to Jesus expressing amazement at someone's faith both involved Gentiles (Matthew 8:10; 15:28). Finally, we find many implicit references to a future Gentile mission (Matthew 4:12-17; 12:18, 21; 21:43; 24:14; 25:32; 26:13). All of this to say, the Gospel is for all people in all places.

What was the historical setting for the writing of Matthew's Gospel? Though we cannot know for certain, the content of the book may help us find the answer. Throughout the Gospel, we see Jesus and the religious establishment in intense conflict. Jesus more strongly condemns the Pharisees and teachers of the law in Matthew 23 (36 verses) than the parallels in Mark (3 verses) and Luke (3 verses). Matthew condemns the Sadducees in equally strong terms (Matthew 3:7; 16:6, 11, 12; 22:23, 34). By comparison, Mark and Luke refer to the Sadducees only one time each. None of the other Gospels attacks the Jewish leadership as harshly as does Matthew's Gospel (Matthew 3:7-10; 5:20; 7:29; 8:11-12; 13:11-17; 16:6, 12; 21:33-45; 22:1-10; 23:2-8, 13-26). Considering the focus on Jesus' condemnation of the religious establishment and its opposition to Jesus, Matthew may have written to Jewish Christians facing similar opposition.

Though it is impossible to date Matthew's Gospel with precision, a date in the 60s is likely. If the Temple had already been destroyed, why would the author fail to mention it as a fulfillment of Jesus' words in Matthew 24? Most scholars believe that Matthew wrote his Gospel from Antioch of Syria. A large Jewish population there became a center of missionary outreach for the apostle Paul. Nothing of importance, however, depends on the Gospel being written in Antioch.

Unlike Luke and John, Matthew states no specific purpose for writing. He may simply have wanted to preserve an accurate account of Jesus' words and deeds for future generations, as the original eyewitnesses began to die off. Considering the content of the Gospel, however, it seems likely he wrote to strengthen his readers' faith in Jesus in the face of rising persecution.

What features make Matthew's Gospel distinctive among the four Gospels? Matthew's emphasis on Jesus as the Son of David and his strong denunciation of the religious leaders stand out. Matthew also shows a keen interest in eschatology (the study of last things). Jesus' Olivet discourse in Matthew (on the destruction of the Temple and Jesus' second coming) is 97 verses long, while it is 37 verses long in Mark and 31 verses in Luke. Of the four Gospels, only Matthew uses the term *parousia* ("coming"), Paul's favorite term to refer to Christ's second coming (Matthew 24:3, 27, 37, 39). Matthew also makes several eschatological references to final judgment. Several times Matthew uses the phrase "weeping and gnashing of teeth" to symbolize eternal punishment (Matthew 8:12; 13:42, 50; 22:13; 24:51; 25:30), while Mark and Luke use it only once apiece. In the parable of the sheep and the goats, the king says to those on his left (the goats), "Away with you, you cursed ones, into the eternal fire prepared for the devil and his demons" (Matthew 25:41).

Matthew also has an ecclesiological interest (ecclesiology is the study of the doctrine of the church). Only Matthew's Gospel uses the word "church" (Greek, *ekklesia*) (Matthew 16:18; 18:17). The structure of the Gospel, with its five blocks of Jesus' teaching, would make it easy for the church to teach (catechize) new believers. Matthew also gives some preliminary instructions on the process of church discipline (Matthew 18:12-20).

Matthew's comprehensive Gospel emphasizes Jesus' discourses, with five large blocks of Jesus' teachings alternating with narrative material.

- Narrative (Matthew 1–4)
- Discourse 1: The Sermon on the Mount (Matthew 5–7)
- Narrative (Matthew 8–10)
- Discourse 2: Mission Discourse (Matthew 10)
- Narrative (Matthew 11–13)
- Discourse 3: Kingdom Parables (Matthew 13)
- Narrative (Matthew 14–17)
- Discourse 4: Community Life (Matthew 18)
- Narrative (Matthew 19–22)
- Discourse 5: Condemnation and Prophecy (Matthew 23–25)
- Narrative (Matthew 26–28)

Each discourse concludes with a phrase like, "When Jesus had finished saying these things" (Matthew 7:28; 11:1; 13:53; 19:1; 26:1). Matthew used these phrases to transition from discourse to narrative material. Matthew's arrangement of the discourses made instructing young believers in the teaching of Jesus very convenient.

Outline

1. The Birth of Jesus the Messiah (Matthew 1:1–2:23)

2. The Words and Works of Jesus the Messiah (Matthew 3:1–18:35)

3. The Journey to Jerusalem of Jesus the Messiah (Matthew 19:1–20:34)

4. The Passion and Resurrection of Jesus the Messiah (Matthew 21:1–28:20)

Digging Into Matthew's Gospel

The Birth of Jesus the Messiah (Matthew 1:1-2:23)

Matthew begins by recounting selected events surrounding Jesus' birth, although technically he never describes the birth itself. The first chapter establishes Jesus' identity. The genealogy retells Israel's history in three stages of fourteen names: from Abraham (the father of the Jewish people) to David (Israel's greatest king); from David to Josiah (Israel's last free king); from Jehoiachin (also known as Jeconiah and the first king during the Babylonian captivity) to the Messiah. The number fourteen is the numerical value of David's name (in Hebrew) and highlights Jesus' connection to David. The main point of the genealogy is to demonstrate that Jesus is the Son of David. Notice the names of five women, a highly unusual practice in a Jewish genealogy.

The remainder of Matthew's narrative on Jesus' birth and infancy is built around five Old Testament quotations (Matthew 1:23; 2:6, 15, 18, 23). These quotations reveal how Jesus' birth and infancy fulfilled key scriptural prophecies. Chapter 1 thus introduces Jesus as the son of Abraham, the son of David, and Immanuel ("God with us"). Chapter 2 discloses that even the places where Jesus lived fulfilled Old Testament prophecies: Bethlehem, Egypt, and Nazareth.

The Words and Works of Jesus the Messiah
(Matthew 3:1-18:35)

In this longest section of the book, Matthew moves from Jesus' infancy to his adulthood. The other Gospels also include a description of the ministry of John the Baptist (Matthew 3:1-12). Matthew describes John's food and clothing in a way reminiscent of the prophet Elijah. Of all the Gospels, only Matthew explains John the Baptist's hesitancy in baptizing Jesus (Matthew 3:13-17). From his baptism, God leads Jesus into the wilderness to confront the devil (Matthew 4:1-11). Only Matthew specifically mentions Jesus relocating to Capernaum and how his Galilean ministry fulfilled the Scriptures (Matthew 4:14-16, cf. Isaiah 9:1-2). Jesus launches his Galilean ministry by calling four disciples (Matthew 4:18-22). Crowds gather around him quickly as he travels throughout Galilee, preaching and performing miracles (Matthew 4:23-25).

Chapters 5–9 demonstrate the authoritative nature of Jesus' teaching in the Sermon on the Mount (Matthew 5–7) and in his powerful miracle-working ability (Matthew 8–9). The Sermon on the Mount is the most famous sermon in the history of the world. In it, Jesus establishes the ethical standards for Kingdom living. One does not live out these truths *to become* a Christian, but Christians desire to live out these truths *by the power* of God's Spirit. We can divide the sermon into three sections: an introduction (Matthew 5:1-16); the body (Matthew 5:17–7:12); and the conclusion (Matthew 7:13-29).

Following the Sermon on the Mount, Matthew presents a series of nine miracle stories (three groups of three, covering ten miracles), interspersed with two examples of Jesus' teaching on discipleship. Unlike Mark, Matthew groups his succinct account of these miracles thematically rather than chronologically. Jesus heals outcasts in the first set of stories (Matthew 8:1-17), followed by a rejected call to discipleship (Matthew 8:18-22). In a second group of miracle stories, Jesus demonstrates his authority over nature, demons, and sickness (Matthew 8:23–9:8). In a second call to discipleship, Matthew contrasts a positive response to discipleship with the pettiness of the Pharisees (Matthew 9:9-17). In a third set of miracle stories, Jesus heals a sick woman, raises a dead girl to life, and heals two blind men and a man rendered mute by demons (Matthew 9:18-34). One may wonder at this point, *How could anyone oppose someone who performs such miracles?*

In preparation for his mission discourse, Jesus tells his disciples that while the harvest is great, the workers are few. Prayer to the Lord of the harvest is the only proper response to a need for workers (Matthew 9:35-38). Matthew then lists the names of the twelve disciples whom the Lord will send out (Matthew 10:1-4). This prepares readers for Jesus' second discourse.

We can divide Jesus' mission discourse into two sections. First, Jesus gives instructions to the Twelve for an immediate "short-term" mission excursion (Matthew 10:5-16). Jesus' instructions focus on teaching the disciples to trust in God's providential care. The remainder of the discourse concentrates on the church's future mission work (Matthew 10:17-42). Jesus does not hide from the disciples that they will encounter great opposition (Matthew 10:17-25); they must fear God and not people (Matthew 10:26-31). Their allegiance to God must supersede every other relationship (Matthew 10:32-42).

After Jesus predicts future opposition, Matthew begins to describe rising opposition to Jesus' ministry. In chapter 11, the opposition seems more implied than overt, but in chapter 12 the opposition becomes obvious. We see some examples of this rising opposition even in John the Baptist, when he asks Jesus, "Are you the Messiah we've been expecting, or should we keep looking for someone else?" (Matthew 11:1-19). Jesus pronounces doom on cities that saw his miracles but refused to believe (Matthew 11:20-24). In chapter 12, the hostility increases significantly. The Pharisees accuse Jesus and his disciples of breaking rabbinical Sabbath regulations (Matthew 12:1-14). They accuse Jesus of being in league with Satan (Matthew 12:22-37). The intensity of opposition continues to rise as the scribes and Pharisees demand that Jesus perform a sign to prove his authority (Matthew 12:38). When Jesus compares his enemies to a house indwelt by a demon (Matthew 12:39-45), he hints that his opponents are more than human. The chapter concludes with a description of those who do the will of God as Jesus' true family (Matthew 12:46-50).

Jesus tells several Kingdom parables explaining the growing chasm between himself and his opponents (Matthew 13:1-52). First, Jesus addresses the crowds (Matthew 13:1-35), and then he speaks privately to his disciples (Matthew 13:36-52). The two longest parables in the discourse are the parable of the sower (Matthew 13:3-9; 16-23) and the parable of the wheat and the tares (Matthew 13:24-30; 36-43). These parables explain part of the reason for the rising hostility to Jesus. Sandwiched between the telling of the parable of the sower and its interpretation is Jesus' explanation of why he teaches in parables, revealing his purpose in his quotation of Isaiah 6:9-10. The parable of the wheat and the tares teaches that as Jesus sows Kingdom seed (the sons of righteousness), the devil sows tares (the sons of the devil).

The parable illustrates the "behind the scenes" battle taking place in Jesus' ministry.

The parables describing opposition to the Kingdom culminate in the rejection of Jesus at Nazareth and Antipas's execution of John the Baptist (Matthew 13:53–14:12). Still, opposition does not stop Jesus from performing astonishing miracles, such as the feeding of five thousand and walking on water. (Peter's role in the story is unique to Matthew 14:13-36.)

Jesus challenges the traditions of the elders and condemns their unholy hearts (Matthew 15:1-20). By contrast, Jesus casts a demon out of a Gentile woman's daughter in response to the woman's faith (Matthew 15:21-28). After another feeding miracle—this time, a crowd of four thousand consisting mainly of Gentiles (Matthew 15:29-39)—Jesus returns to Galilee, where conflict with the Pharisees and Sadducees continues (Matthew 16:1-12). The high point of this portion of the Gospel is Peter's dramatic confession at Caesarea Philippi, followed immediately by Jesus' first passion prediction (Matthew 16:13-28).

On the Mount of Transfiguration, God declares Jesus to be his "dearly loved Son" (Matthew 17:1-9). Later the disciples' failure to cast out a demon provides a teachable moment for Jesus to instruct them on the importance of faith (Matthew 17:14-21). After Jesus casts out the demon, he again predicts his coming death and resurrection (Matthew 17:22-23). The section concludes with the story of Jesus paying the Temple tax, recorded only in this Gospel (Matthew 17:24-27).

Jesus' community discourse focuses on the importance of four major characteristics for healthy community life in the future church: humility (Matthew 18:1-5); holiness (Matthew 18:6-9); a willingness to pursue those who wander from the fold (Matthew 18:10-14); and forgiveness (Matthew 18:15-35).

The Journey to Jerusalem of Jesus the Messiah (Matthew 19:1-20:34)

Jesus leaves Galilee to begin his fateful journey to Jerusalem (Matthew 19:1). He performs few miracles along the way, keeping his focus on his teaching. He covers a significant range of topics, revealing both his wisdom and his depth of scriptural understanding. Topics include marriage, divorce, celibacy (Matthew 19:1-12), children (Matthew 19:13-15), the danger of possessions (Matthew 19:16-26), and the promise of future reward (Matthew 19:27-30). The parable of the vine growers demonstrates God's grace in salvation (Matthew 20:1-16). Jesus' third passion prediction (Matthew 20:17-19) precedes James and John's failure to understand Jesus' teaching on servant leadership (Matthew 20:20-28). This portion of the narrative concludes with the healing of two blind men in Jericho, who identify Jesus as the Son of David (Matthew 20:29-34).

The Passion and Resurrection of Jesus the Messiah (Matthew 21:1-28:20)

Matthew devotes a significant amount of space to the final week of Jesus' life, thus revealing its importance in Matthew's thinking. The week begins with three prophetic acts: the Triumphal Entry; the clearing of the Temple; and the cursing of the fig tree (Matthew 21:1-22). The Temple clearing results in a series of heated exchanges between Jesus and various religious groups (Matthew 21:23-45). At every point, Jesus demonstrates that he is wiser and more insightful than his opponents.

Jesus' fifth discourse divides into two sections. First comes a condemnation of the Pharisees and teachers of the law (Matthew 23:1-36), concluded by Jesus' heartache over Jerusalem's rejection of him (Matthew 23:37-39). Next come predictions of the Temple's destruction and his second coming (Matthew 24:1–25:46). Matthew also gives much space to the final hours of Jesus' life: Chapter 26 begins by contrasting Judas and the religious leaders' plot to kill Jesus, with an unnamed woman anointing him (Matthew 26:1-16). Jesus uses the Passover meal as a window to his impending work on the cross (Matthew 26:17-35). After these events, the pace quickens, beginning with Jesus' agony and arrest in the garden of Gethsemane (Matthew 26:36-56), followed by several trials before the Sanhedrin and the Roman governor (Matthew 26:57–27:31), and culminating in Jesus' crucifixion and burial (Matthew

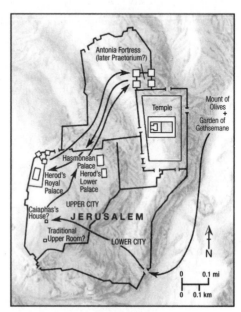

Jesus' Trial

27:32-66). Only Matthew's Gospel describes Judas's suicide (Matthew 27:3-10), an earthquake, and the resurrection of saints (Matthew 27:51-53).

Matthew's resurrection narrative falls into four parts: the women's discovery of the empty tomb (Matthew 28:1-7); the women's encounter with the risen Christ (Matthew 28:8-10); the plot by the religious leaders and the Roman soldiers to explain away the empty tomb (Matthew 28:11-15); and the Great Commission (Matthew 28:16-20).

Living Out the Message of Matthew

All of the most important truths in Matthew are Christological. Matthew's Gospel is first and foremost about Jesus Christ. We see Jesus' significance in that while Jesus is David's Son, he is also David's Lord (Matthew 22:41-46). Jesus is greater than Abraham, as he is the head and founder of a newly formed people of God and the one who will bring God's blessings to all nations (Genesis 12:2-3; 15:4-6; Matthew 28:18-20). Jesus is greater than Moses. Both Moses and Jesus were born in treacherous times (Exodus 1:6-22; Matthew 2:16-20). They both went up on a mountain and brought God's Word to God's people (Exodus 19; Matthew 5–7). Jesus is the greater prophet Moses predicted in Deuteronomy 18:15-18. Jesus brings a new and greater exodus, as he delivers God's people from Satan, sin, and eternal death. In addition, Jesus' resurrection from the dead proves him to be greater than Jonah (Matthew 12:41), and by his teaching, wiser than Solomon (Matthew 12:42). The church's Savior and Lord is worthy of worship and obedience, for the Old Testament Scriptures find their ultimate fulfillment in him.

References to Jesus' abiding presence with his people bookend the Gospel. In chapter 1, Jesus is called "Immanuel, which means 'God is with us'" (Matthew 1:23), and the book concludes with Jesus' promise, "I am with you always, even to the end of the age" (Matthew 28:20). In Matthew 10:40, Jesus tells his disciples, "Anyone who receives you receives me, and anyone who receives me receives the Father who sent me." In the parable of the sheep and the goats, Jesus says, "And the King will say, 'I tell you the truth, when you did it to one of the least of these my brothers and sisters, you were doing it to me!'" (Matthew 25:40). When two or three are gathered in Jesus' name, he is with them (Matthew 18:20). These words would have meant much to a people sent out into a world inhabited by "wolves" to share the Good News (Matthew 10:16). No matter where God's people are, and no matter what happens to them, Jesus has not abandoned them. He is always present with them!

Final words matter, and Jesus' final words in this Gospel give a Great Commission to his disciples to make disciples of all nations. The one who sends the church out into the world has all authority. He not only sends them, but he also goes with them.

2

Mark

Jesus Is the Son of God

FROM BEGINNING TO END, Mark's Gospel moves along like a high-speed train. One of Mark's favorite words is the adverb "immediately," which in the NASB translation he uses forty-one times to keep the Gospel moving quickly from one event to the next.

The Big Picture

The early church unanimously considered the author to be John Mark. Mark was not one of Jesus' twelve disciples, however, so where did he get his information? Ancient church testimony connects John Mark to Peter. Peter mentions Mark in his first epistle: "my son, Mark" (1 Peter 5:13, NASB). Though Mark was not Peter's biological son, he seems to have been a spiritual son to the apostle. The Gospel is built on the solid testimony of Peter, a trustworthy account of Jesus' words and deeds.

Mark likely wrote his Gospel before the other three. Though

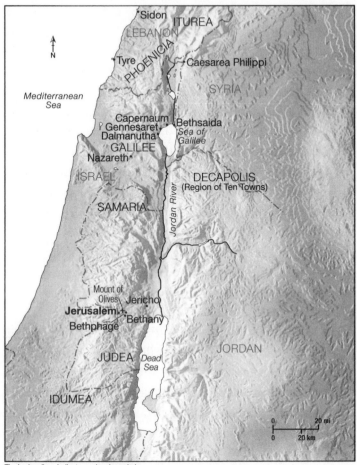

The broken lines indicate modern boundaries.

Key Places in Mark

we cannot date the Gospel with certainty, it was probably written sometime between AD 55 and 65. Scholars generally assume Mark wrote his Gospel from Rome, intending it for Christians in and around Rome, as well as for all believers scattered throughout the world.

Though Mark does not state his purpose for writing, likely

he had a multifaceted objective. First, when Mark wrote, the first followers of Jesus' ministry were dying off. Mark's Gospel provided a historical record for future generations of what Jesus taught and did. Second, considering the space Mark gave to Jesus' final week (Mark 11–16), he probably wrote to demonstrate the importance of Jesus' death and resurrection. The sacrificial death and resurrection of Jesus form the core of the Good News. As the church expanded further into the Gentile world, this information was crucial to gospel proclamation. Third, Mark wrote to highlight the cost for disciples of following Jesus. Mark's Gospel spotlights the failure of the disciples in a way that surpasses the other Gospels— and yet, Jesus did not give up on them. Disciples are not perfect people, but are wholly committed to following Jesus and growing spiritually. Mark's major purpose is to establish that Jesus the Messiah is the Son of God, which he states unambiguously in the opening verse.

Though the Gospels do not mention John Mark by name, the book of Acts does mention him. The first reference comes in connection with his mother's home in Jerusalem, where Peter went after his miraculous release from prison (Acts 12:12). Later, Mark accompanied Paul and Barnabas when they returned to Antioch from a visit to Jerusalem (Acts 12:25). He then went along as an "assistant" to Paul and Barnabas on their first missionary journey (Acts 13:5). Unfortunately, he did not last long as a missionary helper. At Perga in Pamphylia, he left the mission and returned to Jerusalem (Acts 13:13). Paul was strongly opposed to Mark's decision, and when Barnabas suggested that they take Mark with them on their second missionary journey, Paul refused. Barnabas then took Mark, who was his younger cousin (Colossians 4:10), and sailed for Cyprus (Acts 15:36-39). But that is not the end of the story.

Approximately ten years later, we see Mark again with Paul, this time in Rome (Colossians 4:10; Philemon 1:24). By the end of Paul's life, Mark had become a crucial aide (2 Timothy 4:11). Paul's words suggest that in the years between his separation from Barnabas and his first Roman imprisonment, his attitude had changed toward John Mark, likely the result of Barnabas discipling Mark. Peter also spoke of Mark's presence with him and the help Mark had given him in Rome. From what appears to have been a rough beginning, Barnabas's investment in Mark paid great dividends. Mark eventually served alongside both Peter and Paul and wrote the first of the four Gospels.

One important literary feature in Mark's Gospel is the so-called *Markan sandwich*, in which one event gets "sandwiched" between the beginning and ending of another event. The feature follows an A/B/A pattern in which the two related events interpret one another.

We see an example of this in the story of the raising of Jairus's daughter from the dead and the healing of a woman with an issue of blood (Mark 5:21-43). The story begins by recounting Jairus pleading with Jesus to come and heal his daughter. Jairus drops out of the story when an unnamed woman takes the spotlight. She has been ill for twelve years (just as Jairus's daughter is twelve years old). After Jesus heals the woman, the story returns to Jairus and his daughter. Both stories help the reader understand the importance of faith in Jesus during life's most desperate moments.

A second example occurs in Mark's placement of Jesus' clearing of the Temple, between his cursing of the fig tree and the disciples' later discovery of the withered tree (Mark 11:12-25). This arrangement helps the reader understand that just as the tree produced no edible fruit, so the Temple lacked spiritual fruit for God's glory.

Outline

We can divide Mark's Gospel into two large sections. The first section highlights Jesus' powerful deeds and the increasing opposition to him during his Galilean ministry (Mark 1:1–8:26). The second half highlights Jesus' movements toward Jerusalem and his final days in Jerusalem (Mark 8:27–16:8).[3]

1. Jesus the Messiah Is the Son of God (Mark 1:1–8:26)

2. Jesus the Messiah Is the Suffering Servant (Mark 8:27–16:8)

Two important statements and two key events bracket Mark's Gospel. The important statements confess that Jesus is the Son of God. The first of the statements begins Mark's Gospel: "This is the Good News about Jesus the Messiah, the Son of God" (Mark 1:1). The second comes at Jesus' death, when a Roman centurion, after watching Jesus die, says, "This man truly was the Son of God!" (Mark 15:39). The irony of the second confession is that while the centurion spoke better than he knew, Mark's readers know the full depth of the centurion's statement. Elsewhere in the Gospel, other than Jesus himself (Mark 13:32; 14:61-62), only God the Father (Mark 1:11; 9:7) and demons (Mark 3:11; 5:7) refer to Jesus as the Son of God.

The key events bracketing the Gospel are Jesus' baptism, when Jesus saw the heavens "splitting apart" (Mark 1:10), and his death, when the Temple curtain "was torn in two, from top to bottom" (Mark 15:38). The same Greek word is used for the sky "splitting apart" and the "tearing" of the Temple curtain. At Jesus' baptism, the heavens were torn apart and God acknowledged Jesus as his beloved Son. At Jesus' death, the Temple curtain was "torn . . .

from top to bottom," signifying a new opening into God's presence. In his baptism, Jesus identified with sinners; at his death, he died for them.

Digging Into Mark's Gospel

Jesus the Messiah Is the Son of God (Mark 1:1-8:26)

Mark's opening statement introduces his main character, "Jesus the Messiah, the Son of God" (Mark 1:1). First and foremost, Mark's Gospel is about Jesus. After the opening affirmation, Mark moves quickly, mentioning John the Baptist's ministry as the fulfillment of ancient prophecies; Jesus' baptism, where God announces Jesus as his beloved Son; and Jesus' temptations by the devil in the wilderness (Mark 1:2-13). Mark covers a lot of material in the first thirteen verses! Before Mark begins to describe Jesus' Galilean ministry, he summarizes Jesus' message as "the Kingdom of God" (Mark 1:14-15). The Kingdom of God comes in two stages. The arrival of King Jesus inaugurated the Kingdom, and at his return he will consummate the Kingdom.

Jesus begins his Kingdom advancement by calling four fishermen to be his disciples (Mark 1:16-20). Discipleship is integral to Kingdom advancement. Jesus' encounter with a demonized man in a Capernaum synagogue demonstrates that Kingdom advancement will encounter significant opposition by Satan and his demons (Mark 1:21-28).

Powerful miracles and intense conflict characterize Jesus' Galilean ministry. The first half of the Gospel describes fifteen of Jesus' eighteen miracles. In fact, almost 50 percent of the first eight chapters tell stories of how Jesus performed miracles. The chart below indicates Jesus' miracles in Mark's Gospel and the parallels in Matthew, Luke, and John.

JESUS THE MESSIAH, THE SON OF GOD				
	Mark	**Matthew**	**Luke**	**John**
Casting Out an Unclean Spirit	1:23-26		4:33-35	
Healing Simon's Mother-in-law	1:30-31	8:14-15	4:38-39	
Healing a Leper	1:40-45	8:2-4	5:12-14	
Healing a Paralytic	2:1-12	9:2-8	5:17-26	
Healing a Withered Hand	3:1-6	12:9-14	6:6-11	
Stilling the Storm	4:35-41	8:23-27	8:22-25	
Healing the Gadarene Demoniac	5:1-20	8:28-34	8:26-39	
Resurrecting Jairus's Daughter	5:21-43	9:18-26	8:40-56	
Healing the Woman with Constant Bleeding	5:25-34	9:20-22	8:43-48	
Feeding the Five Thousand	6:30-46	14:13-23	9:10-17	6:1-15

	Mark	Matthew	Luke	John
Walking on Water	6:47-52	14:24-32		6:16-21
Healing the Gentile Woman's Daughter	7:24-30	15:21-28		
Healing the Deaf and Dumb Man	7:31-37	15:29-31		
Feeding the Four Thousand	8:1-9	15:32-38		
Healing the Twice-Touched Blind Man	8:22-26			

JESUS THE MESSIAH, THE SUFFERING SERVANT				
	Mark	Matthew	Luke	John
Casting Out a Demon from a Boy	9:14-29	17:14-20	9:37-43	
Healing a Blind Man Near Jericho	10:46-52	20:29-34	18:35-43	
Cursing the Fig Tree	11:12-14, 20-25	21:20-22		

Interspersed throughout these miracles stories we see increasing opposition to Jesus. For example, Mark 2:1–3:6 records a series of conflict stories that help explain why Jesus' enemies hated him. Jesus claimed to forgive sin, a prerogative belonging only to God (Mark 2:1-12); Jesus associated with irreligious people such as the tax collector Levi (Mark 2:13-17); Jesus feasted rather than fasted (Mark 2:18-22); Jesus showed a disregard for rabbinic rules governing the Sabbath, demonstrating himself to be Lord of the Sabbath (Mark 2:23–3:5). Jesus' enemies responded by plotting to kill him (Mark 3:6). His own family thought, *He's out of his mind* (Mark 3:20-21), the scribes thought he was demon-possessed (Mark 3:22), and his hometown of Nazareth did not believe in him (Mark 6:1-6). Jesus knew the heartache and pain of being misunderstood by those who loved him and what it felt like to be hated without a cause!

How could Jesus possibly encounter such opposition, despite all his miracles? The parable of the sower (Mark 14:1-20) helps the reader understand. In the parable, Jesus compares himself to a farmer sowing seed. Some seed fell on hard soil, other seed fell on shallow soil, some on cluttered soil, and still other seed on good soil. These soils represent the various hearts of those who hear Jesus' teaching. The hard soil represents those who, like much of the religious establishment, oppose Jesus. Satan comes and takes away the seed sown on hard hearts (Mark 4:15). Others, like the crowds who have only a shallow commitment to Jesus based on their emotions after witnessing his miracles, begin to follow Jesus but fall away quickly when persecution arises (Mark 4:16-17). Still others have cluttered hearts. The worries of the world, the deceitfulness of riches, and desires for other things eventually choke out the work of the Word in their lives (Mark 4:18-19). But those with hearts like fertile soil respond to Jesus' words (Mark 4:20). These individuals are like the ones described at the end of chapter 3, seated at Jesus' feet, listening to his teaching and putting it into practice (Mark 3:33-35).

The section concludes with the strange miracle story of the twice-touched blind man (Mark 8:22-26). Why was the man not healed the first time Jesus touched him? The story is an "enacted parable," an historical event that serves a purpose like a parable. The story helps the reader understand why the disciples will be unable to fully comprehend Jesus' passion predictions, beginning in the next episode. They understand partially who Jesus is: the long-awaited Messiah. But at this point, they fail to grasp the necessity of his death and resurrection. The disciples' second touch will come at the resurrection. Only then will they begin to see clearly.

Jesus the Messiah Is the Suffering Servant (Mark 8:27–16:8)

The Gospel pivots in a new direction at Caesarea Philippi, where Peter makes his great confession that Jesus is the Messiah (Mark 8:27-30). The opening section focuses on Jesus' journey to Jerusalem, his passion predictions, and calls to discipleship (Mark 8:27–10:52). Three strategically located passion predictions punctuate this section (Mark 8:31-32; 9:30-32; 10:32-34), and each of them immediately precedes a call to discipleship (Mark 8:34-38; 9:33-37; 10:35-45). Interspersed throughout the remainder of this section, Jesus teaches on a wide range of topics (marriage, children, the danger of wealth, and servant leadership), instructing his disciples and the crowds on what it means to live as disciples. This section concludes with the healing of blind Bartimaeus (Mark 10:46-52).

The next section focuses attention on Jesus' final days of ministry in Jerusalem, beginning with the Triumphal Entry on Palm

Sunday and culminating with Jesus' Olivet discourse on Tuesday afternoon (Mark 11:1–13:37). In between these two events, Mark describes a series of encounters between Jesus and his opponents, demonstrating the tremendous chasm between them (Mark 11:27–12:44).

Mark recounts Jesus' final hours with stunning detail (Mark 14:1–15:47). He begins with preparation for the Passover meal and concludes with the burial of Jesus' body. On Thursday evening, Jesus eats the Passover meal with his disciples (Mark 14:12-31). The Passover meal provides a window to Jesus' impending work on the cross. The atmosphere in the room must have grown tense as Jesus predicted one of them would betray him and Peter would deny him. Jesus' agony in the garden of Gethsemane shocks us (Mark 14:32-42). Why would he pray, "Please take this cup of suffering away from me"? Jesus' prayer gives us further insight into his crucifixion. On the cross, he will suffer for people's sins. A mob arrests Jesus in the garden, as if he were a common criminal (Mark 14:43-52). His trials before the Sanhedrin and Pilate mock justice (Mark 14:53–15:15). An innocent man is condemned to death, while a guilty man (Barabbas) goes free. Jesus' only words from the cross recorded by Mark are a cry of abandonment: *"Eloi, Eloi, lema sabachthani?"* which means, "My God, my God, why have you abandoned me?" (Mark 15:34). Mark concludes with a brief but glorious description of a group of women encountering angels at Jesus' empty tomb (Mark 16:1-8).

Living Out the Message of Mark

Mark's Gospel has many important themes relevant to today, but three stand out. The first is Christology. The term *Christology* refers to the study of the person and work of Christ. As we have seen, Mark begins his Gospel with an affirmation that Jesus is the

Messiah and the Son of God. The first half of the Gospel confirms Jesus to be the powerful, miracle-working Son of God, as he heals the sick, feeds the hungry, and raises the dead. At the midpoint of the Gospel, Peter acknowledges Jesus as the Messiah. From that point on, Mark depicts Jesus as Isaiah's Suffering Servant, who gives his life as "a ransom for many" (Mark 10:45). Mark's presentation of Jesus should cause us to fall on our faces in worship. One who could perform the miracles Jesus performed, yet who chose

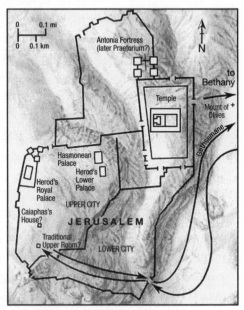

Passover Meal and Road to Gethsemane

to die to redeem sinners, deserves our worship, love, and obedience.

A second important theme is discipleship. In his first act of ministry performed after his baptism and temptation, Jesus called four fishermen to be his disciples. He eventually chose twelve men to pour himself into, and out of those twelve he focused even more attention on three (Peter, James, and John). After each passion prediction, Jesus gave specific instructions about discipleship. Disciples are called to take up their cross and follow Jesus and to seek to serve rather than to be served. Every Christian must take seriously the requirement of discipleship. Jesus does not call perfect people to be disciples—just consider the shortcomings of his own disciples. But every believer *is* a disciple and needs to grow in Christlikeness.

The third key theme is the death of Jesus. As we have seen, approximately 40 percent of the book focuses on Jesus' final week. Mark wants his readers to understand that Christ's death was no mere miscarriage of justice, nor a tragic ending to a life once filled with great potential. God's plan called for Jesus to die. Jesus often referenced his death (Mark 2:19-20; 8:31; 9:31; 10:33-34, 45; 12:1-11; 14:8, 22-25, 27). The Old Testament foretold it (Mark 12:10; 14:49), and the religious leadership looked for an opportunity to arrest and kill Jesus (Mark 3:6; 12:12; 14:1-2). Through all these situations, God clearly remains in control. At no point is Jesus caught unaware of these events. At no point do these events veer outside God's plan or control. Yet, at the same time, those who carried out these evil acts are guilty of their sinful choices. God's plan to redeem for himself a people for his own possession required Jesus' death and resurrection. As Christians grow in their understanding of the Good News, they need a great appreciation for God's love for them, as demonstrated in Christ's cross. Christians have a message of hope for the world. Jesus Christ died for sinners, was raised by God from the dead, and is alive today to offer salvation to all who believe!

own d...... ...., ... believer is a disciple ... . no place
in China......

3

Luke

Jesus Is the Savior of the World

THE GOSPEL OF LUKE is meant for all people. Michael Wilcock
states it well:

> The gospel is not only for Jews, but also for Greeks—and
> for Romans and for Samaritans too. It is not only for
> males, but also for females—and not simply important
> women like the wife of Herod's steward, but widows and
> cripples and prostitutes as well. It is not only for freemen,
> but also for slaves—and indeed for all whom society
> despises: for the poor, the weak, and the outcast, for the
> thief and the quisling. And all of these Luke delights to
> show as particular individuals. A galaxy of such portraits
> glitters across his twenty-four chapters. These are real
> people, and among them the human condition is really to
> be found.[4]

The Big Picture

The early church writers unanimously declared Luke, beloved physician and missionary companion of Paul, to be the author of this Gospel and the book of Acts. As with Matthew's and Mark's Gospels, the superscription ("According to Luke") gives early second century evidence of the church's conviction of Luke's authorship.

Acts contains five "we" passages, where the author describes himself present with Paul (Acts 16:10-17; 20:5-17; 21:1-18; 27:1-29; 28:16). We see this connection between the Gospel and Acts when we consider that Acts picks up where the Gospel ends. In addition, both books are dedicated to Theophilus, both have common themes and theology and a common style of writing and vocabulary. Luke–Acts clearly was written by the same person.

Paul provides a few pieces of background information on Luke. Luke apparently accompanied Paul in his first and second Roman imprisonment (Acts 27:1-29; Colossians 4:14; 2 Timothy 4:10-11). Paul refers to Luke as the "beloved physician" (Colossians 4:14, NASB). These references also tell us that Luke was a Gentile. As a Gentile and not one of Jesus' original followers, we can reasonably assume the early church writers would not have ascribed authorship of these two volumes to Luke if they did not believe he wrote them.

As with Matthew and Mark, it is difficult to precisely date the writing of the Gospel. If the events described in Acts ended before Paul's release from his first Roman imprisonment (AD 62), then likely Luke completed his Gospel sometime around AD 60. If Luke ended Acts where he did because he intended to describe the gospel making its way to Rome, however, then a date as late as the 70s is possible. The earlier date seems more likely.

The broken lines indicate modern boundaries.

Key Places in Luke

Luke wrote his Gospel from Rome. We know that he was in Rome during Paul's first Roman imprisonment (Acts 27:1–28:16). Luke writes primarily for Gentile believers (though not to the exclusion of Jewish Christians) in and around Rome. Luke's Gospel would have been copied and quickly distributed to other churches beyond Rome.

Outline

1. Luke's Prologue (Luke 1:1-4)

2. Jesus' Birth and Infancy (Luke 1:5–2:52)

3. Jesus' Preparation for Ministry (Luke 3:1–4:13)

4. Jesus' Ministry in Galilee (Luke 4:14–9:50)

5. Jesus' Journey to Jerusalem (Luke 9:51–19:27)

6. Jesus' Ministry in Jerusalem (Luke 19:28–24:53)

Digging Into Luke's Gospel

Luke's Prologue (Luke 1:1-4)

The Gospel begins with an explanation of Luke's process in researching and writing. What was his primary purpose in writing? In the prologue, Luke states, "Having carefully investigated everything from the beginning, I also have decided to write an accurate account for you, most honorable Theophilus, so you can be certain of the truth of everything you were taught" (Luke 1:3-4).

Jesus' Birth and Infancy (Luke 1:5-2:52)

In this first major section, Luke spends two chapters alternating between the birth and infancy of John the Baptist and Jesus. As significant as John the Baptist will be as prophet of the Most High God and forerunner to the Messiah, Jesus is always superior as the Son of the Most High God. John's parents are long past their child-bearing years but are miraculously enabled to conceive through the normal relations of a husband and wife. Jesus, by contrast, is conceived by the Holy Spirit through a virgin. We see the events of these two chapters through Mary's perspective, which contrasts with the infancy narrative in the Gospel of Matthew from Joseph's perspective.

Jesus' Preparation for Ministry (Luke 3:1-4:13)

Luke describes the ministry of John the Baptist (Luke 3:1-20) and then Jesus' baptism, genealogy, and temptation (Luke 3:21–4:13). While Matthew begins his Gospel with Jesus' genealogy, Luke waits until chapter 3 to present it. Oddly enough, Luke separates Jesus' baptism and temptation with the genealogy. Rather than beginning the genealogy with Abraham and working toward Jesus, as Matthew did, Luke begins with Jesus and works backward all the way to Adam. In this, Luke has a twofold intention: to connect Jesus to all of humanity through Adam; and to contrast Adam's sin in the Garden with Jesus' victory over Satan in the wilderness.

Jesus' Ministry in Galilee (Luke 4:14-9:50)

Jesus has just come out of the wilderness, "filled with the Holy Spirit's power," and begins his Galilean ministry in Nazareth (Luke 4:14-30). Jesus' Nazareth sermon, and especially his quotation of Isaiah 61:1-2, becomes the lens through which we are to view his ministry. His rejection at Nazareth foreshadows a rocky road ahead. Luke 4:31-44 illustrates Jesus' fulfillment of Isaiah 61:1-2 as Jesus heals the sick and casts out demons in Capernaum.

Discipleship and opposition characterize Jesus' Galilean ministry (Luke 5–6). Luke expands on Mark's description of the calling of the four fishermen by focusing on Peter (Luke 5:1-11). After Jesus heals a man with leprosy (Luke 5:12-16), Luke depicts a series of conflicts between Jesus and his opponents (cf. Mark 2:1–3:6). The conflicts center around Jesus' authority to forgive sins (Luke 5:17-26), his feasting instead of fasting (Luke 5:27-39), and his disregard for rabbinical rules governing the Sabbath day (Luke 6:1-10). The passage concludes on an ominous note: "At this, the enemies of Jesus were wild with rage and began to discuss what to do with him" (Luke 6:11). After a night of prayer, Jesus calls twelve men to be his disciples (Luke 6:12-19). Luke then records Jesus' Sermon on the Plain (Luke 6:20-49). The placement of the discourse seems intended to teach Jesus' disciples how they are to live.

Near the end of chapter 7 we find a crucial question: "Who is this man?" (Luke 7:49). The events preceding the question have prepared readers to answer it. The chapter begins by describing Jesus' ministry to outcasts: He heals a Roman centurion's servant (Luke 7:1-10) and raises a widow's son from the dead (Luke 7:11-17). The crowd reacts with joy, saying, "A mighty prophet has risen among us" and "God has visited his people today" (Luke 7:16).

John the Baptist sends his disciples to ask Jesus, "Are you the Messiah we've been expecting, or should we keep looking for someone else?" (Luke 7:19-20). Jesus responds by recounting his miracles and reminding them that the Good News is preached to the poor (Luke 7:22). The religious leaders answer the same question by calling Jesus "a glutton and a drunkard, and a friend of tax collectors and other sinners!" (Luke 7:34). The chapter concludes at a dinner party in the home of a Pharisee, where Jesus pronounces forgiveness of an immoral woman's sins (Luke 7:36-50). Those sitting at the table ask, "Who is this man, that he goes around forgiving sins?" (Luke 7:49).

After a brief interlude in which readers learn that Jesus and the disciples are financially supported by a group of devout women (Luke 8:1-3), Jesus teaches in parables (Luke 8:4-21). Luke's parable discourse is much shorter than the parallels in Matthew and Mark, apparently because Luke reserves most of his parables for the later travel narrative (Luke 9:51–19:27). The main point of this section of parables is to demonstrate that authentic hearing leads to obedient faith (Luke 8:21).

Jesus' parabolic teaching precedes three miracle stories (with four miracles), demonstrating Jesus' authority over nature, demons, sickness, and death. In the first story, Jesus calms a storm on the Sea of Galilee (Luke 8:22-25). The disciples respond by asking, "Who is this man?" The answer: He who has authority over nature. The next story gives a second answer: He who causes a legion of demons to tremble (Luke 8:26-39). The demons know his identity and call him "Son of the Most High God" (Luke 8:28). The intertwined third and fourth miracle stories (Luke 8:40-56) show Jesus healing a woman with an issue of blood and raising a dead girl to life. Who is Jesus? One who has authority over nature, demons, sickness, and death.

Chapter 9 continues to reveal the identity of Jesus. The chapter begins with Jesus sending out the Twelve on a short-term mission excursion (Luke 9:1-6). In response to Jesus and the disciples' ministry, Herod Antipas concludes Jesus must be John the Baptist, raised from the dead, while others think Jesus might be Elijah or another prophet risen from the dead (Luke 9:7-9). Shortly after Jesus feeds the 5,000 (Luke 9:10-17), Peter confesses Jesus to be "the Messiah sent from God!" (Luke 9:20). Jesus immediately defines his Messiahship in terms of rejection, death, and resurrection (Luke 8:21-27).

About eight days later, Jesus takes his inner circle (Peter, John, and James) up on a mountain to pray (Luke 8:28-36). Jesus is transfigured before their eyes, and he speaks with Moses and Elijah about his coming "exodus." Now a voice from heaven answers the question about Jesus' identity: "This is my Son, my Chosen One. Listen to him" (Luke 9:35). Listen to him about what? About what he has said about his death and resurrection. After casting a demon out of a boy (Luke 9:37-43), Jesus makes his second passion prediction (Luke 9:44-45). Jesus concludes his Galilean ministry by teaching the disciples about the importance of servant leadership (Luke 9:46-50).

Jesus' Journey to Jerusalem (Luke 9:51-19:27)

The longest section in the Gospel, spanning almost ten chapters, involves Jesus' journey to Jerusalem. Luke mentions it several times (Luke 9:51; 13:22; 17:11; 19:11, 28). Much of the material in this section is unique to Luke's Gospel. It focuses on teaching, especially about discipleship (Luke 11:1-13; 13:18-30; 14:25-35; 16:16-31; 17:1-10, 20-37). Of the twenty miracles in Luke's Gospel, we find only four in the travel narrative (Luke 13:10-17; 14:1-4; 17:11-19; 18:35-43). Of the twenty-three parables in Luke's Gospel, we find sixteen in this section. Of those sixteen parables, three topics stand out: prayer (Luke 11:1-13; 18:1-8, 9-14); the use of financial resources (Luke 12:16-21; 16:1-13, 19-31); and ministry to outcasts (Luke 14:15-24; 15:1-32).

During this season, Jesus focuses much of his teaching on preparing the disciples for ministry after his ascension. At the same time, Luke disciples his readers to be people of prayer, to use their financial resources for Kingdom purposes, and to minister to those on the fringes of society. We find some of Jesus' most famous parables in this section: the Good Samaritan; the Prodigal Son; the persistent widow; and the unrighteous steward, to name a few. Before reaching Jerusalem, Jesus stops in Jericho, where he heals a blind beggar and Zacchaeus comes to faith in Jesus (Luke 18:35–19:10). Jesus speaks one final parable before entering

Jerusalem, designed to prepare his followers for his absence (Luke 19:11-27).

Jesus' Ministry in Jerusalem (Luke 19:28-24:53)

Luke concludes his Gospel with Jesus' passion in Jerusalem. Passion week begins with Jesus' triumphal entry into Jerusalem on Palm Sunday (Luke 19:28-44). Luke's report of Jesus' entry includes a few features unique to his account. When the Pharisees insist that Jesus quiet the crowd, Jesus replies, "If they kept quiet, the stones along the road would burst into cheers!" (Luke 19:39-40). Luke also includes an account of Jesus weeping over Jerusalem and prophesying its future destruction (Luke 19:41-44; cf. Matthew 23:47). Unlike Mark, who describes Jesus returning to Bethany after looking around the Temple precinct, Luke cuts to the chase and describes Jesus clearing the Temple (which took place on Monday, Luke 19:45-48). Instead of the Temple being a place dedicated to God's glory, the religious establishment had turned it into a flea market.

On Tuesday of Passion week, Luke narrates Jesus' conflict with his enemies (Luke 20:1-40). Each time, Jesus' wisdom and his depth of understanding of the Scriptures confound his opponents. Finally, Jesus turns the tables on those questioning him (Luke 20:41-47). Quoting from Psalm 110:1, Jesus asks how David's son can be both Messiah and David's Lord. Before they can answer, Jesus condemns the teachers of the religious law. Luke's three-verse summation sounds quite severe (Luke 20:45-47).

The final event before Jesus leaves the Temple takes place in the court of the women (Luke 21:1-4), where Jesus commends the generosity and great faith of a poor widow. Luke's placement of this event sharply contrasts this humble widow with the arrogant teachers of the law.

As Jesus and his disciples leave the Temple, some of the disciples admire its grandeur. Once again, Jesus predicts the destruction of the Temple in the near future (a fact that was fulfilled in AD 70), and he also speaks of his Second Coming in the distant future (Luke 21:5-36).

On Wednesday, Judas enters the city alone and arranges with the Jewish leadership to betray Jesus (Luke 22:1-6). Luke details Jesus' instructions for preparation for the Passover meal, the institution of the Lord's Supper, the prediction of betrayal, teaching on servant leadership, and a prediction of Peter's denials (Luke 22:7-38).

From this point on, events unfold quickly: Jesus prays on the Mount of Olives and then is arrested, brought before a Jewish tribunal, and convicted of blasphemy. Shortly after the break of dawn, soldiers drag Jesus before the Roman governor, Pontius Pilate, who eventually convicts him of insurrection (Luke 22:39–23:25). Only Luke describes Jesus' appearance before Herod Antipas (Luke 23:7-12).

Luke records three of Jesus' seven final sayings on the cross: "Father, forgive them, for they don't know what they are doing" (Luke 23:34); "I assure you, today you will be with me in paradise" (Luke 23:43); "Father, I entrust my spirit into your hands!" (Luke 23:46). Jesus is buried before sunset on Friday afternoon (Luke 23:50-56).

Luke has the longest resurrection narrative among the synoptic Gospels (Luke 24:1-53), and Luke's vignette of Jesus and two disciples on the road to Emmaus is the longest story in his Gospel. The length of the story reveals its importance in Luke's thinking (Luke 24:13-34). The two most important theological concepts in Luke's resurrection narrative are the physicality of Jesus' resurrection (Luke 24:15-16, 36-43) and how it fulfilled

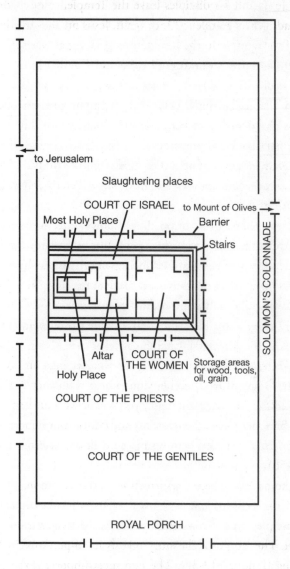

to Jerusalem

Slaughtering places

COURT OF ISRAEL

to Mount of Olives →

Most Holy Place

Barrier

Stairs

SOLOMON'S COLONNADE

Altar

COURT OF
THE WOMEN

Storage areas
for wood, tools,
oil, grain

Holy Place

COURT OF THE PRIESTS

COURT OF THE GENTILES

ROYAL PORCH

The Temple in Jesus' Day

Scripture (Luke 24:25-27; 44-48). Only Luke fully describes Jesus' ascension, which he does in both Luke 24:50-53 and Acts 1:9-11.

Living Out the Message of Luke

Luke's major themes reveal matters close to his heart, and many of these themes continue to have great importance for believers today. Luke demonstrates a great interest in people, an interest we can trace back to Jesus himself. Luke introduces his readers to several individuals not mentioned in Matthew or Mark: Zechariah and Elizabeth, Simeon and Anna, Mary and Martha, Zacchaeus, Cleopas and his unnamed companion on the road to Emmaus, and many others. In addition, Luke shows Jesus' heart for outcasts like Zacchaeus, the chief tax collector; an unnamed immoral woman, who anointed his feet; and a Samaritan, the only one of ten lepers who thanked Jesus for healing them.

Luke highlights the important role women played in Jesus' ministry, from Mary, Elizabeth, and Anna in the birth and infancy narratives, to the women watching at Jesus' crucifixion (who also visited the empty tomb while the male disciples went into hiding). Luke 8:1-3 reveals how several women helped financially support Jesus and the twelve. We learn from all these accounts that Jesus cared about people from every class and background. Luke makes it abundantly clear that Jesus came "to seek and save the lost." If seeking and saving the lost was Jesus' passion, then how much more should it also be our passion?

The prayer life of Jesus is another key theme. Luke depicts Jesus praying more than any of the other Gospels do. In fact, Luke portrays Jesus praying at every important moment in his life. Calling Jesus a man committed to prayer is one thing, but seeing Jesus constantly in prayer is another. At Jesus' baptism, only Luke describes Jesus praying as he was baptized (Luke 3:21). Luke writes in 5:16,

"Jesus often withdrew to the wilderness for prayer." Before Jesus chose the Twelve, he spent the entire night in prayer (Luke 6:12). Before Jesus asked the Twelve who they thought he was, he had been praying (Luke 9:18). About a week later, only Luke describes Jesus praying on the Mount of Transfiguration (Luke 9:29). Luke 10:21-22 records the actual words Jesus prayed.

In Luke 11:1-13, Jesus' disciples ask him to teach them to pray. In the upper room, Jesus tells Peter that Satan has demanded permission to sift him like wheat, but Jesus has interceded for Peter, that his faith would not fail (Luke 22:31-32). In the garden of Gethsemane, Jesus twice tells his disciples to pray so they will not fall into temptation (Luke 22:40, 46). On the cross, Jesus' first and last words were prayers (Luke 23:34, 46).

We focus on this tour of Jesus' prayer life so we can feel the impact of his commitment to prayer. Each reference reinforces the thought that Jesus did not believe he could "do life" without prayer. As God incarnate, why did the Son of God need to pray? Luke does not tell us, but the fact that Jesus often did pray should inspire us to seek to become people of prayer.

A third key theme is the ministry of the Holy Spirit. From the beginning of his Gospel, Luke signifies the important role of the Spirit. John the Baptist was filled with the Spirit while still in Elizabeth's womb (Luke 1:15). The virginal conception resulted from the Spirit's work in Mary's life (Luke 1:35). Both Elizabeth and Zechariah were filled with the Spirit (Luke 1:41, 67). The Spirit guided Simeon into the Temple at the precise moment when he could encounter the baby Jesus (Luke 2:25-27). The Spirit descended in bodily form on Jesus at his baptism (Luke 3:22). Jesus was full of the Spirit and led by the Spirit into the wilderness to confront Satan (Luke 4:1). He came out of the wilderness in the power of the Spirit (Luke 4:14). In his Nazareth sermon,

Jesus declared that the Spirit of the Lord was upon him and had anointed him (Luke 4:18). He rejoiced in the Holy Spirit (Luke 10:21). He warned against blasphemy of the Spirit (Luke 12:10). He promised the Father would give the Holy Spirit to those who asked (Luke 11:13). He told the disciples before his ascension to wait in Jerusalem for power from on high (Luke 24:49), which happened at Pentecost (Acts 2:1-4). God's people need the empowerment of the Spirit if they are to make an impact in this world for Jesus.

The most important theme in Luke may be the theme of salvation. Luke concludes the story of the conversion of Zacchaeus with the statement, "For the Son of Man came to seek and save those who are lost" (Luke 19:10). We see the importance of salvation in the parables of the lost sheep, the lost coin, and the lost son (Luke 15:1-32). We see the same theme in the Temple, when Simeon declares, "I have seen your salvation, which you have prepared for all people. He is a light to reveal God to the nations, and he is the glory of your people Israel!" (Luke 2:30-32). Jesus promises the thief on the cross, "I assure you, today you will be with me in paradise" (Luke 23:43).

Indeed, Jesus is the Savior of all people. Whether they have wealth like Theophilus and Zacchaeus, are immoral like the woman who anointed his feet, or anyone in between, Jesus came to seek and to save.

4

John

Jesus Is God

YOU CAN SAY ALMOST ANYTHING you want about Jesus in today's culture, except that he is God. Jesus' deity is as controversial today as it was in the first century, yet that is exactly what John's Gospel insists about Jesus. His Gospel is not a series of stories haphazardly strung together, but a powerful presentation of the most glorious life ever lived. John's Gospel offers readers the mature reflections of the last living apostle.

The Big Picture

As in the synoptic Gospels, the author of John's Gospel does not name himself. The superscription ("According to John"), however, provides strong, early evidence for Johannine authorship. The consistent testimony of early church writers also supports John's authorship of the fourth Gospel. Scholars generally agree that John wrote his Gospel in approximately AD 85, at or near Ephesus.

Though John does not mention himself by name in the Gospel, the writer does refer to himself as "the disciple Jesus loved" (John 13:23; 19:26; 20:2; 21:7, 20). John was one of Jesus' first followers and a part of Jesus' inner circle (Mark 1:16-20; 5:37; 9:2; 14:33). John and his brother, James, appear to have had fiery dispositions, as Jesus called them "Sons of Thunder" (Mark 3:17). Toward the end of John's life, the Romans exiled him to the island of Patmos (Revelation 1:9).

A major theme in John's Gospel is the deity of Jesus. John states clearly his belief in Jesus' divinity in the opening and closing lines of his prologue (John 1:1-2, 18). John demonstrates Jesus' deity in the Gospel by describing seven miraculous signs Jesus performed. John calls these miracles "signs" because they point to truths about Jesus. As you read John's Gospel, look for how these signs highlight Jesus' identity. The seven signs are: turning water into wine (John 2:1-12); healing a nobleman's son (John 4:43-54); healing a lame man (John 5:1-15); feeding the five thousand with just a few loaves and fish (John 6:1-14); walking on the water (John 6:16-21); restoring sight to a man born blind (John 9:1-7); and raising Lazarus from the dead (John 11:40-44).

John also reveals the deity of Jesus through seven "I am" statements. These "I am" statements point to various aspects of Jesus' divinity: "I am the bread of life" (John 6:35); "I am the light of the world" (John 8:12; 9:5); "I am the gate" (John 10:7, 9); "I am the good shepherd" (John 10:11, 14); "I am the resurrection and the life" (John 11:25); "I am the way, the truth, and the life" (John 14:6); and "I am the true vine" (John 15:1, 5). John wants to make sure his readers understand that Jesus is God!

While Jesus' deity is a key theme in the book, John also has

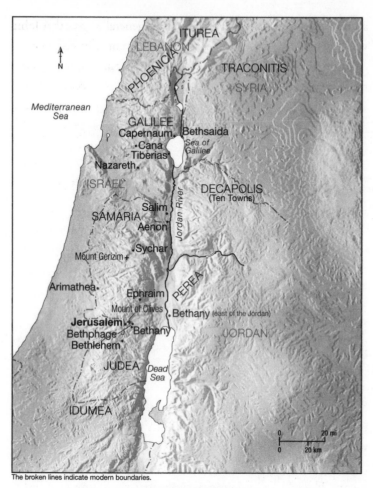

The broken lines indicate modern boundaries.

Key Places in John

other important themes in mind. Those who believe in Jesus receive "eternal life." Eternal life is a relationship with Jesus, which begins in this life and continues throughout eternity. Another important term in the Gospel is the verb "believe." John uses the verbal form ninety-eight times. John plainly states his purpose in 20:30-31: "The disciples saw Jesus do many other miraculous signs in addition to the ones recorded in this book. But these are written so that you may continue to believe that Jesus is the Messiah, the Son of God, and that by believing in him you will have life by the power of his name."

John accomplishes his purpose in the stories he recounts, highlighting both Jesus' words and deeds. With every story, statement, sign, and sermon, John wants his readers to know that Jesus is the Messiah, the Son of the living God.

Outline

This Gospel falls quite naturally into three large sections: Jesus' public ministry, where John presents Jesus' signs and sermons (John 1–12); Jesus' private ministry to the disciples in the upper room, where he washes their feet and gives them important teachings (John 13–17); and Jesus' passion ministry, where John recounts Jesus' trials, crucifixion, and resurrection (John 18–21).

1. Jesus' Public Ministry (John 1:1–12:50)

2. Jesus' Private Ministry (John 13:1–17:26)

3. Jesus' Passion and Resurrection Ministry (John 18:1–21:25)

Digging Into John's Gospel

Jesus' Public Ministry (John 1:1-12:50)

The prologue to John's Gospel sets forth in dramatic fashion the deity of Jesus Christ (John 1:1, 18). The prologue is the lens through which we read the rest of the Gospel. Many of the Gospel's most important themes get introduced here (light, darkness, truth, witness, and world). John applies the title "the Word" to Jesus in the prologue but nowhere else in his Gospel. We find the background to the term in the Old Testament, where God's word is the dynamic force of his will (Genesis 1:3; Psalm 33:6; Isaiah 55:11). Although the Gospel does not mention Jesus by name until verse 17, the opening lines make it clear that Jesus is the Word.

The remainder of chapter 1 confirms John's testimony about Jesus in the prologue. In John 1:19-34, we hear the testimony of John the Baptist. Jesus is the Lamb of God, the one who baptizes in the Holy Spirit, and the Chosen One of God. In John 1:35-51, we hear the testimony of some of Jesus' earliest followers, who call him Rabbi, Messiah, the one of whom Moses and the prophets wrote, Son of God, King of Israel, and Son of Man. As the first chapter ends, Jesus' identity is unmistakable.

The next section of the Gospel begins at John 2:1 and goes through John 4:54. The opening story takes place in Cana, where Jesus performs his first sign (John 2:1, 11). The final story takes place in Cana once more (John 4:46), where Jesus performs a second sign (John 4:54). Thus, John brackets off chapters 2–4 as a major unit of his Gospel. The key themes in this section are newness and superiority.

In chapter 2, Jesus turns water into wine and clears the Temple. These two events indicate that Jesus is inaugurating a new age (the Messianic age) and Jesus is the new temple (the sacrificial system is coming to an end). In John 3:1-21, Jesus discusses with Nicodemus the necessity of being born again, indicating that Nicodemus, too, needs a new birth. Later, in the exchange between John the Baptist and his disciples, Jesus is clearly portrayed as superior to John the Baptist (John 3:22-36). Jesus' encounter with the Samaritan woman and the villagers from her town reveals a new outreach of the gospel beyond the confines of Judaism (John 4:1-42). The final story in this section describes the healing of an official's son, revealing Jesus as the giver of new life (John 4:43-54).

In the next major section of the Gospel, John shows how Jesus fulfills and exceeds many of the Jewish holy days and festivals (John 5:1–10:42): the Sabbath (John 5:1-47); Passover (John 6:1-71); Tabernacles (John 7:1–10:21); and Dedication (John 10:22-42). Many of Jesus' signs and sermons relate to one another in this section: the healing of the blind man (John 5:1-9) and the divine Son discourse (John 5:19-30); the feeding of the five thousand (John 6:1-15) and the Bread of Life discourse (John 6:35-59). Jesus demonstrates that he is the light of the world (John 8:12; 9:5) in the healing of the blind man (John 9).

Throughout this larger section, we see rising hostility toward Jesus. After the healing of the blind man, Jesus calls God his Father, making himself equal to God (John 5:17-18). As a result, the Jewish leaders want to kill him (John 5:18). After the Bread of Life discourse, many of his followers abandon him (John 6:66). In chapter 7, his brothers taunt him (John 7:1-5), Jesus is accused of being demon possessed (John 7:20), and an attempt to arrest him fails (John 7:32, 45). In chapter 8, the rising tensions increase. Jesus is accused of being a demon-possessed Samaritan (John 8:48). As the chapter ends, the Jews pick up stones to throw at him (John 8:59). In chapter 9, the Pharisees call Jesus a sinner because he heals a blind man on the Sabbath day (John 9:16). The section concludes in Jerusalem with another attempt to stone Jesus (John 10:31).

The transitional chapters of 11–12 describe the final days of Jesus' public ministry: the resurrection of Lazarus from the dead (John 11:1-44); Mary's anointing of Jesus (John 12:1-11); Jesus' triumphal entry into Jerusalem (John 12:12-19); and Jesus' final public words (John 12:20-50).

Jesus' Private Ministry (John 13:1-17:26)

Without John's Gospel, we would know very little of what Jesus taught his disciples in the upper room on the night before his crucifixion. The farewell discourse is Jesus' final teaching to his disciples before his arrest. They must have spent several hours together that night. He begins in stunning fashion by revealing the meaning of his work on the cross and, in washing their feet, the power of humble service (13:1-17). He identifies Judas as his betrayer and predicts Peter's denials (13:18-38).

In John 14:1-31, much to the disciples' surprise, Jesus teaches that it would be better for him to depart than to remain with them. In John 15:1-17, Jesus teaches the beautiful truth of the mutual indwelling of Christ in the believer and the believer in Christ, using the imagery of a vine and its branches. Those who remain in Christ demonstrate their relationship to him by loving fellow believers. His disciples need to know that persecution lies in their future, but they will never have to face it alone (15:18–16:4). Jesus returns to the theme of his departure in John 16:5-33. Despite his leaving, Jesus encourages the disciples that he will send the Spirit to turn their grief into joy and ensure their ultimate victory, despite tribulation.

Jesus' upper room ministry to the disciples concludes with prayer for his disciples and future believers (John 17:1-26)— Jesus' longest recorded prayer in the Bible. It can be divided into three sections. Jesus first prays for himself, not in a selfish way but that the Father would be glorified in him (17:1-5). Second, Jesus prays for his disciples (17:6-19). This portion of the prayer can be divided into three thoughts: Jesus gives a progress report on his disciples (17:6-8); he prays for their spiritual protection (17:9-12); he prays that they would be set apart for world missions (17:13-19). Lastly, Jesus prays for future believers (you and me!) (17:20-24).

Jesus' Passion and Resurrection Ministry (John 18:1-21:25)

John 18:1–19:42 records events beginning with Jesus' arrest in the garden and culminating with his death and burial. Jesus' greatness is reflected as he moves toward the Cross with a great sense of purpose and resolve. Jesus' courage and bravery provides an example for his followers about how to endure the persecution he said would come. John's Passion narrative contains four major scenes. First, the events begin in a garden across the Kidron Valley, where Jesus is arrested (John 18:1-11). Second, the scene then shifts to an interrogation before Annas, the father-in-law of the high priest (John 18:12-14, 19-24). While Jesus is interrogated inside Annas's home, outside in the courtyard Peter denies his relationship to Jesus (John 18:15-18, 25-27). Jesus' trial before Pilate, the third scene, is the most extensive (John 18:28–19:16). Much of this material is unique to John's Gospel. The final episode describes Jesus' crucifixion and burial (John 19:17-42). John's Gospel has three of Jesus' famous seven last words. John also shows how, after Jesus' death, the Scriptures continue to be fulfilled (Exodus 12:46; Zechariah 12:10).

John describes four major events in chapter 20. In the first event, Mary Magdalene discovers the empty tomb, followed by an examination by Peter and an unnamed disciple (John 20:1-10). Second, John describes Mary's dramatic encounter with the risen Jesus (John 20:11-18). Third, Jesus appears to the disciples during Thomas's absence (John 20:19-23). Fourth, Jesus appears a week later to the disciples with Thomas present (John 20:24-29). The chapter concludes with John's purpose in writing his Gospel (John 20:30-31).

The final chapter of John's Gospel serves as something of an epilogue, in which John recounts experiences that explain and affirm Jesus' ministry (John 21:1-25). First, he describes another miraculous catch of fish in the Sea of Galilee (John 21:1-14), an event very similar to one that occurred when Jesus first called Peter, Andrew, James, and John to become fishers of men (Luke 5:1-11). This second miraculous catch reminds them of their calling. Next, he recounts Peter's reinstatement as leader of the Twelve (John 21:15-23). Three times Peter denied Jesus, and three times Jesus asks Peter if he loves him. Jesus calls Peter to love, service, and death. Lastly, John affirms the truthfulness of his Gospel's witness (John 21:24-25).

Living Out the Message of John

John's Gospel focuses on the deity of Jesus Christ. Not only did Jesus exist before Abraham (John 8:58), but Jesus has *always* existed (John 1:1-2). Jesus is our creator, redeemer, and Lord. Considering what John teaches about Jesus, we must recognize Jesus' absolute supremacy over all of life.

The twenty-first-century church must recapture a vision of the glory and splendor of Jesus Christ. The contemporary church's vision of Jesus is far too small, made evident in our lack of passion in worship and our hesitancy in evangelism. When a church catches a glimpse of Jesus' greatness, her members sing loudly and they willingly sacrifice time, money, and life to take the gospel to the nations. This vision of the glory of Christ motivated members of the early church to willingly lay down their lives for the expansion of God's Kingdom.

5

Acts

"To the Ends of the Earth"

THE BOOK OF ACTS BEGINS where the Gospel of Luke ends. In an ancient bookstore, Luke's Gospel and Acts would have stood side-by-side on the shelf. Eugene Peterson captures the thought beautifully: "Luke continues his narration with hardly a break—a pause perhaps to dip his pen in the inkwell—writing in the same style, using the same vocabulary."[5] Luke connects his Gospel to Acts with his opening line, "Dear Theophilus, in the first volume of this book I wrote on everything that Jesus began to do and teach" (Acts 1:1). The word *began* indicates Luke's intention to continue the story of Jesus. In his Gospel, Luke portrays Jesus' earthly ministry. In Acts, he describes Jesus' heavenly ministry through the Holy Spirit in the lives of his followers.

Acts provides an essential historical bridge between the Gospels

Key Places in Acts

and the Epistles. Without Acts, we would know little of Paul's relationship with the churches to whom he wrote. For example, Acts 16:11-40 describes Paul planting the church in Philippi, which helps readers better understand Paul's letter to the Philippians. The same is true of many of Paul's other epistles.

The book of Acts inspires readers to trust in God to do great things through ordinary people. From a small beginning, the gospel makes its way to the city of Rome. When ministers and missionaries feel discouraged, they should read Acts and feel inspired by what God can do through ordinary people.

The Big Picture

Luke's authorship of Luke–Acts is generally recognized. Both books are addressed to Theophilus. They have common themes, a similar writing style, and a shared vocabulary. Luke traveled with Paul during some of his journeys. Acts contains five "we" sections written during the author's travels with Paul (Acts 16:10-17; 20:5-17; 21:1-18; 27:1-29; 28:16).[6]

Acts covers a period of approximately thirty years (AD 30–62), beginning in the days leading up to Jesus' ascension and concluding with Paul's two-year Roman imprisonment. The ending of Acts suggests that when Luke completed his book, Paul remained incarcerated. If Paul was still in prison, then Acts was written in approximately AD 62. If Luke intended to trace the progress of the gospel from Jerusalem to Rome, however, then the book could have been written anytime in the 60s or 70s (cf. Acts 1:8). A date of AD 62 is slightly more probable.

The major purpose for writing Acts can be found in Luke's Gospel: "Having carefully investigated everything from the beginning, I also have decided to write an accurate account for you, most honorable Theophilus, so you can be certain of the truth of everything you were taught" (Luke 1:3-4). Luke wanted his readers to know the historical circumstances surrounding the gospel's advancement "to the ends of the earth" (Acts 1:8). Secondary purposes can be discerned by recognizing major themes in the book.

As you read through Acts, notice several important topics. Note every time prayer is mentioned, for example. Luke's Gospel highlights Jesus as a man of prayer. In the same way, Luke wants readers of Acts to understand that the church must continue to pray. Second, examine closely the preaching of Peter, Paul, and Stephen. Approximately twenty percent of Acts recounts sermons and speeches. Observe similarities in the sermons preached to Jewish audiences, especially as they highlight Jesus' fulfillment of the Old Testament. Sermons preached to pagan audiences, by contrast, begin very differently. But both kinds of sermons end with solid gospel presentations.

Observe also the ministry of the Holy Spirit. As you read Acts, underline every reference to the Holy Spirit. The pervasive ministry of the Spirit reminds us that human ingenuity cannot advance the Kingdom.

Outline

Acts can be outlined in several ways. First, we could break down the book into two large sections, based on the ministries of Peter and Paul. In Acts 1–12, Peter is the primary character; in Acts 13–28, Paul takes center stage. Comparing the ministries of the two apostles shows God clearly at work through both.

A second approach tries to understand the book as organized around a series of similar phrases intended to indicate the conclusion of one section and the beginning of the next. Acts 6:7 provides an example: "So God's message continued to spread. The number of believers greatly increased in Jerusalem, and many of the Jewish priests were converted, too" (Acts 9:31; 12:24; 16:5; 19:20; 28:31).

A third approach sees Acts 1:8 serving as a table of contents for the book: "But you will receive power when the Holy Spirit comes upon you. And you will be my witnesses, telling people about me everywhere—in Jerusalem, throughout Judea, in Samaria, and to the ends of the earth." This third approach guides our discussion of content.

1. The Church in Jerusalem (Acts 1:1–7:60)

2. The Gospel Spreads and the Church Expands into Judea and Samaria (Acts 8:1–12:25)

3. The Gospel Spreads and the Church Expands to Rome (Acts 13:1–28:31)

Digging Into Acts

The Church in Jerusalem (Acts 1:1-7:60)

These chapters describe events in and around Jerusalem in the early years of the church. After giving a summary of the third Gospel, Luke recounts the forty days of Jesus teaching his followers and describes his ascension (Acts 1:1-11). The remainder of the chapter focuses on a description of the death and replacement of Judas (Acts 1:12-26).

Chapter 2 details events that occurred on the Day of Pentecost (Acts 2:1-41)—a lot of space is devoted to a single day. But this event fulfills Jesus' promise that his followers would be baptized in the Holy Spirit (Acts 2:1-4; cf. Acts 1:5). As a crowd gathers, Peter seizes the opportunity to preach, and three thousand people come to faith in Jesus (Acts 2:14-41). Acts 2:42-47 offers a programmatic summary of life in the early years of the Jerusalem church. Acts 3:1–6:7 offers representative vignettes illustrating the programmatic summary: miraculous healings through the apostles (Acts 3:1-10); a second sermon by Peter (Acts 3:12-26); and persecution (Acts 4:1-23; 5:12-42). Chapter 4 concludes with an example of the church's care and ministry to its members (Acts 4:32-37).

We see the first sign of struggle within the church in the duplicity of Ananias and Sapphira (Acts 5:1-11). Peter makes clear Satan's involvement in their sin (Acts 5:3). Satan will do anything to stop the expansion of the gospel, whether through persecution from outside the church or moral compromise from within it. Most of chapters 6 and 7 narrates Stephen's sermon and martyrdom. Stephen's death results in widespread persecution, prompting Hellenistic Jewish Christians to flee Jerusalem, taking the gospel with them.

The Gospel Spreads and the Church Expands into Judea and Samaria (Acts 8:1-12:25)

Philip also fled Jerusalem, taking the gospel with him. In Acts 8:4-40, he preaches the gospel to Samaritans and to a Jewish proselyte, an Ethiopian eunuch. The gospel begins to tear down racial barriers.

Acts 9 recounts Saul's conversion on the road to Damascus and subsequent events, culminating with his return to Tarsus. Stephen (Acts 7), Philip (Acts 8), and Saul (Acts 9) all play important roles in the gospel's expansion: Stephen by his death; Philip by his evangelization of the Samaritans; and Saul by his travels and ministry to Gentiles in far-flung areas.

Chapters 10–12 narrate the gospel's expansion to the Gentiles. The amount of space Luke gives to telling the story of the conversion of Cornelius, a Roman army officer, demonstrates its importance (Acts 10:1–11:18). Furthermore, Cornelius's conversion results from the ministry of Peter, the apostle to the Jews, rather than from Paul, the apostle to the Gentiles. The fact that Peter, rather than Paul, led Cornelius to faith means the Jerusalem church was less likely to question the Gentile's conversion.

Luke then describes how the gospel makes its way to Antioch (Acts 11:19-30). The church at Antioch becomes the sending church for Paul and Barnabas on their first missionary journey. Believers are first called Christians at Antioch. Chapter 12 concludes this section of the book with the execution of James the apostle, the miraculous release of Peter from prison, and the death of Herod Agrippa (Acts 12:1-25). From here on, the book will focus on the ministry of Paul.

The Gospel Spreads and the Church Expands to Rome (Acts 13:1-28:31)

Chapters 13–28 trace Paul's three missionary journeys to his imprisonment in Rome. During this period, Paul writes most of his letters. The first journey takes Paul and Barnabas from Antioch to Cyprus, Pamphylia, southern Galatia, and back to Antioch (Acts 13:1–14:28). Upon his return, Luke recounts the famous Jerusalem conference (Acts 15:1-35). One of Paul's missionary principles becomes clear on this journey: He begins in the synagogue of each city, concluding that Jews and Gentile God-fearers would be more open to learning about the Messiah. When the synagogues reject the gospel, he turns directly to the Gentiles.

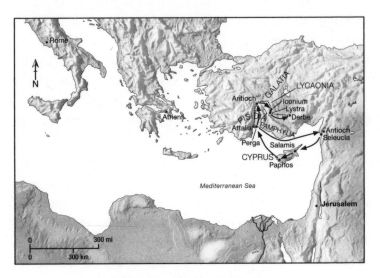

Paul's First Missionary Journey

In Acts 15:36–18:22, Luke narrates Paul's second missionary journey. Paul, along with Silas, returns to Syria and Cilicia, Derbe, and Lystra. At Lystra, Timothy joins the pair, and soon becomes like a son to Paul. After traveling through Asia Minor to Troas, Paul crosses the Aegean Sea to Macedonia. From there he goes to Philippi, Thessalonica, Berea, Athens, and Corinth. Luke gives a great deal of space to Paul's ministries in Philippi and Corinth. The conversions of Lydia and an unnamed jailer, as well as the exorcism of a demon from a slave girl, highlight the apostle's time in Philippi (Acts 16:11-40). Paul spends eighteen months in Corinth (Acts 18:1-18) and from there writes two letters to the church at Thessalonica. The missionary team then returns to Antioch after visiting Jerusalem. One of Paul's mission strategies becomes evident on this journey. He typically plants churches in large urban centers and allows the gospel to reach outlying areas from there.

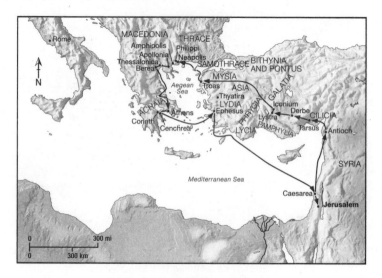

Paul's Second Missionary Journey

Paul spends much of his third missionary journey in Ephesus (Acts 18:23–19:40). From Ephesus, he writes his first letter to the Corinthians, and he may have also written Galatians (though it's possible he wrote that letter from Antioch after his first missionary journey).

Luke details much information on Paul's time in Ephesus (Acts 19:1–41), including his encounter with followers of John the Baptist. Paul exercises a ministry so powerful that even pieces of his clothing, when laid on the sick, result in their healing. Luke also tells us of a botched exorcism by Jewish exorcists, young converts burning their magical paraphernalia, and a violent riot. After leaving Ephesus, Paul returns through Macedonia (where he writes 2 Corinthians), Greece (where he writes Romans), and along the coast of Asia Minor, eventually arriving in Jerusalem (Acts 21:17).

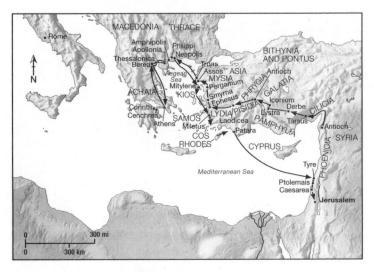

Paul's Third Missionary Journey

In Acts 21:26–26:32, Luke describes Paul on trial before a Jewish mob, another trial before the Roman governors Felix and Festus, and a final hearing before King Agrippa II. At every opportunity, Paul shares the gospel. Luke reproduces much of Paul's defense speeches in this section, likely because Luke accompanied Paul during this time.

Though Acts 27:1–28:16 seems only to trace Paul's journey to Rome, it plays an important theological role. Luke wants to show

how nothing can stop God's will: not a storm at sea, not a secretive plot by soldiers to kill the prisoners, not a shipwreck, not even a poisonous snake bite. Nothing will thwart God's sovereign plan to take Paul to Rome.

The book concludes with Paul preaching the gospel in Rome. During this time, Paul likely wrote his Prison Epistles (Colossians, Philemon, Ephesians, and Philippians).

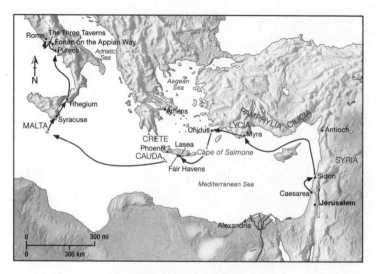

Paul's Journey to Rome

Living Out the Message of Acts

The book of Acts explores some important themes relevant to the twenty-first-century church. One major issue in interpreting Acts is discerning what is normative for the church today and what is merely descriptive, a relatively easy task in the Gospels, where we read of Jesus doing things like walking on water and multiplying a few pieces of bread and fish to feed thousands. No one understands his actions there to be normative for the church today.

Making the same determination in Acts is not nearly so easy. For example, should the church pool its resources and allow church leaders to distribute them to those in need, as the early church did (Acts 2:44-45; 4:32-37)? Is this practice normative or descriptive?

Immediate context is the place to begin to answer this question. In Acts 5:1-11, Ananias and Sapphira die for not sharing the income they gained from selling some land. Peter tells Ananias they were free to sell the land or keep it. If they sold the land, they could give all the money, a portion of the money, or none of the money. What they could not do was pretend to give all the money while holding back a portion of it (Acts 5:4). They committed the sins of lying, hypocrisy, and greed. In the rest of Acts, we do not find the practice of selling possessions and the elders distributing the money outside the Jerusalem church. Neither does the epistolary literature advocate this practice, although the epistles do teach the practice of generosity (cf. 2 Corinthians 8–9).

Why did the Jerusalem church pool its resources? We may find the answer in events on the Day of Pentecost, when several thousand people were saved. Many of these people came to the city as pilgrims to celebrate the festival. Some no doubt wanted to remain in Jerusalem to learn more about their newly discovered salvation. Where would they live, and how would they be fed? The Jerusalem believers took the drastic measures of pooling and selling their possessions to care for one another. We do not learn of similar situations outside of Jerusalem, nor do we see a similar kind of communal sharing elsewhere in Acts. Rather, the church at large followed the principle of generosity and care for fellow believers.

The ministry of the Holy Spirit is one of the most important themes in Acts. Almost every chapter in Acts mentions how God's people need the Spirit's presence in their lives to successfully live the Christian life and fulfill the Great Commission. A difficult interpretive issue in Acts is how to understand the reception of the Spirit in Acts 2, 8, 10, and 19. Jesus instructs his disciples to wait in Jerusalem until they are baptized in the Holy Spirit (Acts 1:5). The coming of the Spirit on the Day of Pentecost fulfills that promise. Two similar events occur later in Acts. In Acts 8, Samaritan believers receive the Spirit after Peter and John lay their hands on them, even though they already had been baptized in water. A comparable event occurs at Cornelius's conversion (Acts 10:1–11:18). As Peter preaches the gospel to Cornelius's household, these Gentiles receive the Holy Spirit. This time, however, no one lays hands on them, nor have they been baptized in water.

How are we to understand these events? Are they normative or descriptive? I believe we should understand them as descriptive rather than normative. First, these events do not follow a similar pattern. Acts 2:1-4 fulfilled Jesus' promise of his followers being baptized in the Spirit. On the Day of Pentecost, believers did not lay hands on one another or pray for one another to receive the Spirit. The Spirit came on them suddenly, but not totally unexpectedly. In Acts 8, the Samaritans trusted in Christ and were baptized in water. Only after the arrival of Peter and John from Jerusalem did they receive the Spirit. In Acts 10, as Peter preached, Cornelius and his household trusted in Christ and the Spirit came upon them as he had at Pentecost. Later they would be baptized in water. Luke does not mention that Peter laid his hands on them. Peter himself reported this event to the Jerusalem leadership:

> "As I began to speak," Peter continued, "the Holy Spirit
> fell on them, just as he fell on us at the beginning. Then I

thought of the Lord's words when he said, 'John baptized
with water, but you will be baptized with the Holy Spirit.'
And since God gave these Gentiles the same gift he gave
us when we believed in the Lord Jesus Christ, who was I
to stand in God's way?"

ACTS 11:15-17

What do we learn from these passages? In chapter 2, Jewish
believers received the Holy Spirit in fulfillment of Jesus' promise.
In Acts 8 and 10, when both Samaritans and Gentiles received the
Spirit, Peter was present and so could authenticate their genuine
reception of the Spirit. In this case, God was tearing down racial
barriers, thus helping early Jewish believers to understand the universal nature of the Church. Acts 19:1-7 should not be understood
as an exception. John the Baptist's disciples did not receive the
Spirit until after Paul preached the gospel to them. They had been
disciples of John the Baptist but had not yet come to faith in Jesus.
The clear teaching in these passages, in the rest of Acts, and in the
epistolary literature, is that believers receive the Spirit at salvation
(1 Corinthians 12:13).

Another theme is the reality of spiritual warfare in gospel
advancement. Satan filled the heart of Ananias to lie to the Holy
Spirit (Acts 5:1-11). Simon the magician hindered the ministry
of Philip (Acts 8:5-25). Elymas likewise attempted to disrupt the
ministry of Paul in Cyprus (Acts 13:6-12). In Philippi, Paul cast
a demon out of a slave girl who had become a distraction (Acts
16:16-18). Paul encountered significant demonic opposition in
Ephesus (Acts 19:8-22). Satan knows his time is short, and he will
oppose the church at every turn.

Despite satanic opposition, the Spirit-filled believers advanced
the gospel from Jerusalem to Rome. The book concludes with Paul

preaching the gospel while under house arrest in Rome. As twenty-first-century believers, reading about the Spirit's work in the book of Acts encourages us to trust God to use us as "gospel lights" in whatever setting he chooses.

PART II

The Letters of Paul

READERS SELDOM CONTEMPLATE why Paul's letters appear in their current order. They are arranged first as letters to churches, from the longest letter (Romans) to the shortest (2 Thessalonians). Next comes letters to individuals, from the longest (1 Timothy) to the shortest (Philemon).

A chronological/theological overview of the Pauline letters shows they can be divided into four groups. Paul's eschatological epistles make up the first group.[7] Eschatology is the study of last things. In the Thessalonian letters, Paul writes much about the Second Coming. Though Paul's original letter did not include chapter and verse divisions, his repeated references in 1 Thessalonians to Christ's return occur at what became the conclusion of every chapter. Both 1 Thessalonians (4:13–5:11) and 2 Thessalonians (1:5–2:12) feature lengthy, significant passages focusing on the Second Coming. Paul wrote these two letters from Corinth on his second missionary journey in approximately AD 50–51.

Paul's soteriological epistles include Galatians, Romans, and the two letters to the Corinthians. Soteriology is the study of salvation. These letters highlight Paul's teachings on justification, sanctification, and glorification. Paul wrote them all on his third missionary journey, although some scholars believe Paul wrote Galatians from Antioch, shortly after he completed his first missionary journey (see discussion of Galatians in chapter 9). He wrote Galatians and 1 Corinthians from Ephesus, 2 Corinthians from Macedonia, and Romans from Corinth. Paul's third missionary journey lasted from approximately AD 52 to 56.

Paul's Prison Epistles include Ephesians, Colossians, Philemon, and Philippians. The apostle wrote them from Rome during his first Roman imprisonment (AD 60–62). Paul wrote the first three early in his imprisonment, while he wrote Philippians last, shortly before his release. Most of us find it difficult to imagine that Paul wrote them all during the many years he spent in prison. Ephesians and Colossians express Paul's cosmic Christology— Jesus is Lord over all the cosmos. In Philemon, Paul appeals to his friend to treat the runaway slave, Onesimus, as a brother in Christ. Philippians teaches the possibility of experiencing joy in all of life's circumstances.

Paul wrote his Pastoral Epistles last, penning 1 Timothy and Titus after his release from his first Roman imprisonment and writing 2 Timothy during his final Roman imprisonment, shortly before his death. He wrote them all between AD 62 and 67, likely writing 1 Timothy from Macedonia (1 Timothy 1:3), Titus from Nicopolis (Titus 3:12), and 2 Timothy from a Roman prison. We call them the Pastoral Epistles because they give extensive instruction on the function and organization of the church. The Pastoral Epistles highlight Paul's love for the Good News and the church, even to the very end of his life.

6

Romans

The Righteousness of God

ROMANS MAY BE the most important letter ever written. It appears first in the series of Paul's letters in the New Testament because of its length, but its primary placement also makes sense because of the letter's impact on the church. No other book in the Bible gives a clearer and more sustained presentation of the Good News than Romans.

The Big Picture

Biblical scholars do not question Paul's authorship of Romans. The letter claims to be written by Paul (Romans 1:1), and no serious challenge to Pauline authorship has ever been made. Tertius probably served as Paul's *amanuensis*—a scribe who wrote what the apostle dictated—and he mentions himself in 16:22. Paul probably sent the letter from Corinth, near the conclusion of his third missionary journey, circa AD 5–56 (Acts 20:3; 2 Corinthians 13:1, 10; Romans 16:1-2, 23).

Paul had several reasons for writing to the church at Rome. First, he wanted to prepare them for his upcoming visit and explain why he had not visited them earlier (Romans 1:8-15). Second, he desired to strengthen the church spiritually (Romans 1:11, 13). Third, Paul appeared concerned about his upcoming visit to Jerusalem (Romans 15:31). If something happened and he did not make it to Rome, he wanted them to understand the gospel he preached. Finally, he wrote to express his hope that they would assist him on his journey to Spain (Romans 15:24, 28).

As you read Romans, look for several key features. Paul lays a doctrinal foundation (Romans 1–11) and then builds practical Christian living upon it (Romans 12–16). The doctrinal section is proportionately longer in Romans than in Paul's other letters because he wants the church to grasp the details of the gospel. Observe how many weighty doctrinal issues Paul handles in chapters 1–11: the wrath of God; universal guilt and condemnation; justification by faith; propitiation; redemption; sanctification; glorification; and Israel's past, present, and future. Recognize how Paul makes significant use of the Old Testament in portions of the epistle (see Romans 3:10-18; 4:1-25; 9:1–11:36). Despite the mind-boggling variety of issues Paul handles, the book has a simple structure.

Outline

1. Man's Desperate Need and God's Glorious Provision in Christ (Romans 1:1–4:25)

2. Union with Christ and the Work of the Spirit (Romans 5:1–8:39)

3. Israel's Past, Present, and Future as a Defense of God's Faithfulness (Romans 9:1–11:36)

4. Carrying Out the Gospel as a Living Sacrifice (Romans 12:1–16:27)

Digging Into Romans

Man's Desperate Need and God's Glorious Provision in Christ (Romans 1:1-4:25)

In the first four chapters, Paul details humanity's desperate need and God's glorious provision in Christ. The first seventeen verses serve as Paul's introduction, the longest of any of Paul's letters. He is attempting to build some rapport with a church he has never visited. The letter explains how God makes us right with himself—how we gain the righteousness of God (Romans 1:16-17). The key Old Testament text for Paul's gospel proclamation in Romans 1:17 comes from Habakkuk 2:4.

Before Paul explains the Good News, he paints a dark, foreboding picture of God's wrath on everyone outside of Christ (Romans 1:18–3:20). He begins by explaining God's wrath upon the Gentile world (Romans 1:18-32). In his systematic presentation, he describes the revelation of God's wrath (Romans 1:18-19) and how God's revelation of himself to all people and their rejection of that revelation provides the basis for his wrath (Romans 1:20-23). Humanity, therefore, is without excuse. We see the execution of God's wrath in the repeated phrase, "God abandoned them" (Romans 1:24, 26, 28).

Paul then turns from the Gentile world to the Jewish world (Romans 2:1–3:8). His argument unfolds in three steps. First, God's judgment is based on truth (Romans 2:1-5), according to every person's deeds (Romans 2:6-11); it is universal (Romans 2:12-16). Second, Paul demonstrates how his Jewish kinsmen have failed to live up to their privileges of having the law and the sign of circumcision (Romans 2:17-29). These verses sound like what Paul may have preached in Jewish synagogues and explains why he met such resistance there. Third, Paul answers Jewish objections to his argument (Romans 3:1-8). After arguing that both Gentiles and Jews stand under God's wrath, Paul strings together a series of Old Testament quotations to substantiate his claims (Romans 3:10-18). *All* people stand under God's wrath because *all* people have sinned. The quote, "No one is righteous—not even one" sums up Paul's thinking (Romans 3:10).

Paul's words, "But now God," transitions to one of the most important passages in the Bible (Romans 3:21-31). Paul explains how people can be made right with God based on the work of Christ, not human effort (Romans 3:21-26). One receives right standing with God by faith (Romans 3:27-31). Abraham serves as Paul's chief example to show that justification has always come through faith—not through works, circumcision, or obedience to the Law (Romans 4:1-16). In addition, just as Abraham believed that God could give life to his and Sarah's "dead" bodies, so Christians believe God gave life to Christ's dead body (Romans 4:17-25).

Union with Christ and the Work of the Spirit
(Romans 5:1-8:39)

In the second major section, we learn that the believer's union with Christ makes possible both holy living and future glory (Romans

5:1–8:39). Justification results in peace with God and a secure hope for vindication on Judgment Day (Romans 5:1-11). The believer's union with Christ, who reversed the effects of Adam's sin, provides the ground of this hope (Romans 5:12-21). Verse 18 captures the essence of this passage: "Yes, Adam's one sin brings condemnation for everyone, but Christ's one act of righteousness brings a right relationship with God and new life for everyone."

In chapter 6, Paul explains that justification by faith alone gives no excuse to sin. The chapter can be divided into two sections. First, the believer's union with Christ means Christians are dead to sin and alive to God in Christ Jesus (Romans 6:1-14). Sin no longer enslaves them, which does not mean they will not sin, but only that their union with Christ has broken the power of sin in their lives. The second half of the chapter approaches the same subject in a slightly different way (Romans 6:15-23). A person is either a slave to sin, resulting in death, or a slave to righteousness, resulting in life. Each of us falls into one of these two categories.

Paul sets forth the thought of chapter 7 in two distinct sections. The first section asserts the believer's freedom from the law and its condemnation (Romans 7:1-13). One should not think that the law is sin, however. The law is not sin, but "the law itself is holy, and its commands are holy and right and good" (Romans 7:12). God's law reveals sin and condemns it (Romans 7:7-13), but obedience to the law could never become the means of salvation.

The second half of the chapter has sparked much controversy (Romans 7:14-25). Interpreters typically fall into one of two camps. One group understands Paul to describe the experience of a non-Christian, while the other understands the passage to describe the experience of a Christian. Those who understand Paul to describe the experience of an unregenerate person point to verse 14: "So the trouble is not with the law, for it is spiritual and good. The trouble is with me, for I am all too human, a slave to sin." They suggest this passage could not refer to a believer. Those who take this passage to describe the experience of a Christian point to verse 22: "I love God's law with all my heart," and argue that an unconverted person would never speak in this way. I find one of the strongest pieces of evidence for understanding this passage to refer to a Christian in Paul's use of present tense verbs in verses 14-25, in contrast to his use of past tense verbs in verses 7-13. Though space does not permit a detailed exposition of the passage, the passage has much in common with Galatians 5:16-25. The Christian is not a slave to sin, but still must battle indwelling sin. Sanctification is a lifelong process.

Romans 8 stands in stark contrast to Romans 7. Whereas chapter 7 mentions the Spirit only once, in chapter 8 the Greek word for "spirit" (*pneuma*) occurs twenty-one times—more than in any other chapter in the New Testament. The chapter may be divided into four sections, each of which gives some facet of the believer's life in the Spirit.

First, life in the Spirit brings a life of victory over indwelling sin (Romans 8:1-8) and death (Romans 8:9-11). Second, life in the Spirit means a life of adoption and heirship (Romans 8:12-17). Adoption points to the believer's present relationship with God and heirship to the promise of future glory. Third, life in the Spirit offers a life of hope for future glorification (Romans 8:17-30). In this section, Paul especially wants to encourage his readers in their present suffering. In verses 19-22, Paul explains his cosmic soteriology. Believers can feel encouraged to know that the cosmos will share in future glory. The chapter concludes in grand fashion: Life in the Spirit makes possible a life of security (Romans 8:31-39). In this section, Paul asks five questions, intended to give believers a deep sense of security not based on emotions but on God's gracious disposition toward them (Romans 8:31-33), on Christ's redemptive work (Romans 8:34), and on God's unchanging love for his people (Romans 8:35-39).

Israel's Past, Present, and Future as a Defense of God's Faithfulness (Romans 9:1–11:36)

The third major section of the book answers the question: "Can God be trusted to keep his promises?" If nothing can separate believers from the love of God (Romans 8:38), then what about his relationship with the Jewish people? Paul's argument unfolds in three stages. Though these chapters have much to say about God's dealings with Israel, Paul writes them to encourage and challenge the church. Broadly speaking, chapter 9 focuses on God's past dealings with Israel, chapter 10 with God's present dealings with Israel, and chapter 11 with God's future dealings with Israel.

Paul has a deep burden for his kinsmen (Romans 9:1-6). He longs to see them come to saving faith. Election characterizes Israel's past (Romans 9:6), and God's election has a discriminating character, as illustrated by the examples of Isaac and Ishmael, and Jacob and Esau (Romans 9:7-13). Nor is God's sovereignty inconsistent with his justice and mercy (Romans 9:14-23). God has extended his grace to both Gentiles (Romans 9:24-26) and for now, to only a remnant of Jews who are being saved (Romans 9:27-29).

The next section focuses on Israel's current disobedience (Romans 9:30–11:10). God's sovereignty is fully compatible with human responsibility. Israel heard the gospel and most Israelites rejected it, but God continues to work with a remnant, Paul being one example (Romans 11:1).

In Romans 11:11-32, Paul explains Israel's future. If God has used Israel's rejection of the gospel for the good of the Gentiles, then Israel's return to God will bless the world (Romans 11:11-15). God's dealings with Israel should warn the Gentiles and encourage them to faith and humility (Romans 11:16-24). God has not finished with Israel and will do a great work in them by incorporating them into the church of Christ (Romans 11:25-32). The concluding doxology brings a fitting end to the entire doctrinal section of the book (Romans 11:33-36).

Carrying Out the Gospel as a Living Sacrifice (Romans 12:1-16:27)

In Romans 12:1–15:13, Paul describes how the gospel transforms human lives. The opening verses of this section lay the groundwork for what it means to be transformed by the renewing of one's mind (Romans 12:1-2). A transformed life reveals itself in the humble use of one's spiritual gifts (Romans 12:3-8), in loving acts of service and hospitality (Romans 12:9-16), by obeying Jesus' teaching concerning love of enemies (Romans 12:17-21), by rendering to Caesar what belongs to Caesar (Romans 13:1-7), by loving one's neighbor as oneself (Romans 13:8-10), by looking toward Christ's second coming (Romans 13:11-14), and by pursuing peace between the weak and the strong (Romans 14:1–15:13). To conclude his book, Paul presents his travel plans, sends greetings to various people, warns about false teachers, offers some personal comments, and pronounces a concluding benediction (Romans 15:14–16:27).

Living Out the Message of Romans

Some people see doctrine as boring and not very relevant. Romans, however, teaches the critical importance of sound doctrine. What a person believes about the gospel determines whether they will go to heaven or hell. If a person focuses only on the love of God to the exclusion of the wrath of God, they will have a distorted understanding of God. When a person understands they are no longer slaves to sin because of their union with Christ, they will subdue the flesh with its passions and desires. Paul's teaching in Romans clearly declares that believers need to understand doctrine if they are to live for God's glory.

The doctrine of justification by faith provided the impetus for the Protestant Reformation. The doctrine of justification teaches that a person is forgiven of their sins and reckoned righteous in Christ at the moment of salvation. People are saved by faith and not by works. A clear grasp of the gospel enables a person to live securely, passionately, and productively in Christ.

7

1 Corinthians

Twenty-First-Century Problems in a First-Century Church

PAUL PLANTED THE CHURCH at Corinth on his second missionary journey. The apostle spent eighteen months there making sure the church began on a solid foundation. The church at Corinth would both greatly bless Paul and give him much consternation. His relationship with the church eventually generated several letters and three visits.

In many ways, 1 Corinthians is one of the most relevant of Paul's letters regarding pastoral theology. He handles an astounding range of issues, including congregational factions; sexual immorality; litigation between members; various views on marriage, divorce, and celibacy; Christian freedom; spiritual gifts; doubts over the future bodily resurrection of believers; and still other issues. The congregation at Corinth was a first-century church with twenty-first-century problems.

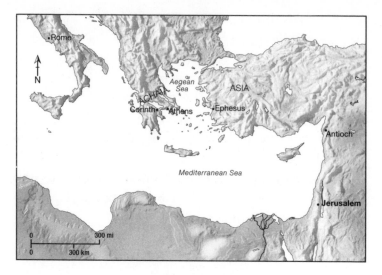

Corinth and Ephesus

The Big Picture

Corinth stood at the southwest end of the isthmus that connects the northern and southern parts of Greece. Corinth's location made it a perfect maritime setting, allowing it to become a significant commercial center. Though the Greco-Roman world was immoral according to Jewish and Christian standards, Corinth had a reputation as an exceptionally immoral city, even among pagans. As the capital of Achaia, Corinth also became an important political city. Religiously, Corinth had multiple temples devoted to various gods and goddesses. One of the most important temples was dedicated to the worship of the Greek goddess Aphrodite, the ancient Greek deity of beauty and sexual love. The Romans called her Venus. The significant worship of Aphrodite within the city may have contributed to Corinth's reputation as deeply immoral.

Evangelical scholarship widely accepts Pauline authorship

of 1 Corinthians. Paul wrote 1 Corinthians from Ephesus on his third missionary journey (1 Corinthians 16:8, 19), likely between AD 54 and 55. He wrote the epistle because of a letter the Corinthians had written him, asking a series of questions on various topics (1 Corinthians 7:1). He also wanted to investigate reports concerning problems in the church (1 Corinthians 1:11). Paul wrote the letter to answer the Corinthians' questions and to address the various matters reported to him.

As you read 1 Corinthians, notice how Paul addresses a wide range of topics, problems as relevant for the contemporary church as they were to the Corinthian church.

Outline

1. Introduction (1 Corinthians 1:1-9)

2. Paul's Response concerning Problems in the Church (1 Corinthians 1:10–6:20)
   a. Factions within the Church (1 Corinthians 1:10–4:21)
   b. Moral Problems within the Church (1 Corinthians 5:1–6:20)

3. Paul Answers Questions from the Corinthians (1 Corinthians 7:1–16:4)
   a. Questions concerning Marriage (1 Corinthians 7:1-40)
   b. Questions concerning Christian Freedom (1 Corinthians 8:1–11:1)
   c. Questions concerning Corporate Worship (1 Corinthians 11:2–14:40)

     d. Questions concerning the Resurrection of the Dead (1 Corinthians 15:1-58)

     e. Questions concerning the Jerusalem Offering (1 Corinthians 16:1-9)

4. Conclusion (1 Corinthians 16:10-24)

Digging Into 1 Corinthians

Introduction (1 Corinthians 1:1-9)

Although it becomes clear quickly that many serious problems plague the church, Paul begins his letter by praising God for the divine grace that has transformed the lives of the Corinthians. God's grace manifests itself in the spiritual giftedness of its members (1 Corinthians 1:4-9).

Paul's Response concerning Problems in the Church (1 Corinthians 1:10–6:20)

Paul had received word that the church had divided into cliques, based on which minister each group championed (1 Corinthians 1:10–4:21). Paul calls such division sinful, since no man can take the place of Christ. These divisions reflect the Corinthians' misunderstanding of the gospel (1 Corinthians 1:18–3:4). Many Corinthians downplayed the power of God and exalted human wisdom. For Paul, God's wisdom far exceeds the best of human wisdom. The world will always view the message of the Cross as foolishness (1 Corinthians 1:18) and the cross of Christ as weakness. But the preaching of the Cross demonstrates both the wisdom and power of God (1 Corinthians 1:19–2:16).

The Corinthian divisions also revealed a false understanding of the Christian minister (1 Corinthians 3:4–4:5). Where the

Corinthians exaggerated the importance of human leadership in the work of the gospel, Paul sets forth his own view of ministry: Ministers are God's servants (1 Corinthians 3:5). Even though Paul and Apollos have different tasks, they are united as servants of the Lord, charged with explaining the mysteries of God (1 Corinthians 4:1-5). The divisions uncover a form of pride and arrogance among the Corinthians, which Paul contrasts with the humility and self-sacrifice of the apostles (1 Corinthians 4:6-13).

The Corinthian church had significant moral issues that Paul needed to address directly. The first, sexual immorality, involved a form of incest (1 Corinthians 5:1-13). Though incest is abhorrent on its own, the Corinthians' prideful boasting brought an even greater humiliation. Paul commands that the immoral man be put out of the church for its protection and, he hopes, for the restoration of the offender.

Paul next addresses the issue of members taking one another before secular courts (1 Corinthians 6:1-11). If Christians will one day participate in the final judgment of the world, Paul says, they ought to be competent to handle internal disputes among themselves (1 Corinthians 6:2). Such a litigious mindset indicates deeper spiritual issues. It is better to be wronged than to allow the gospel to suffer shame.

Last, Paul addresses the issue of Christian freedom and sexual immorality (1 Corinthians 6:12-20). Freedom in Christ does not mean the freedom to sin. Christian standards of sexual purity run counter to the world's standards. The believer's body is the temple of the Holy Spirit, and Christians should live accordingly. Paul's message to the Corinthians on the imperative of moral purity applies equally to the church today.

Paul Answers Questions from the Corinthians
(1 Corinthians 7:1-16:4)

The second major section of the letter turns to a discussion centered on questions from the Corinthians. In chapter 7, Paul handles a series of queries concerning marriage (1 Corinthians 7:1-40) and establishes some basic principles related to marriage and celibacy (1 Corinthians 7:1-9). The second issue concerns the permissibility of divorce (1 Corinthians 7:10-24). His instructions on this topic remain as relevant and helpful today as in his own day. Paul then offers some personal advice. Since only a short time remains, believers must use their time in ways that will best enable them to serve God (1 Corinthians 7:25-40).

Chapters 8–10 deal with the larger issue of Christian liberty, while discussing the specific question of whether Christians should eat meat sacrificed to idols. Almost all meat for public sale in Corinth had been dedicated to idols, thus the question arose, could Christians freely eat such meat? Paul concludes that eating at a temple feast places an individual in danger of involvement with demons (1 Corinthians 10:14-22). Food purchased in the market is permitted, however, and the decision to eat food at a non-ceremonial occasion in the privacy of one's home remains a personal choice, based on conscience (1 Corinthians 10:25-30).

Paul's discussion of the Corinthians' situation helps us to ponder matters related to Christian freedom today. In considering the issue of Christian liberty, three principles should guide us. First, love for others must guide Christian freedom (1 Corinthians 8:1-13). Second, a concern for the gospel should guide Christian freedom (1 Corinthians 9:1-23). Third, one's spiritual well-being must guide Christian freedom (1 Corinthians 9:24–10:30). The clear overarching principle insists, do all for the glory of God

(1 Corinthians 10:31). Both Christ and Paul lived consistently by this principle (1 Corinthians 10:32–11:1).

Paul next addresses questions related to Christian worship: the role of men and women in public worship; the Lord's Supper; and spiritual gifts (1 Corinthians 11:2–14:40). Paul first addresses the distinction between men and women in public worship services (1 Corinthians 11:2-16). Since God ordained the distinctive roles of men and women, congregational worship should reflect these distinctives (1 Corinthians 11:3). This order does not indicate the superiority of one gender over the other, but rather shows God's plan to provide structure and order for the home and church.

Next, Paul addresses issues associated with the Lord's Supper (1 Corinthians 11:17-34). Part of the problem centered around a communal meal preceding the Lord's Supper. The way the Corinthians conducted this meal showed a lack of concern for one another. Paul reminds them that sharing the Lord's Supper recalls Christ's work on the cross and anticipates Christ's return. Participation in the Lord's Supper is no trivial matter! God expects his people to prepare themselves spiritually when they participate in the Lord's Supper.

Paul moves on to issues concerning spiritual gifts (1 Corinthians 12:1–14:40). The Corinthians apparently had some confusion over the exercise and nature of spiritual gifts. To help illustrate the essential diversity that creates the oneness of the church, Paul uses an analogy of the human body (1 Corinthians 12:12-31). The church, like the human body, is one and yet made up of many members. The members of the church, with their diverse gifts, are like the parts of the body, mutually dependent and sharing concern for one other. All of this highlights the vast importance of love that acts as a safeguard for the use of spiritual gifts (1 Corinthians 13:1-13).

Though some in the congregation seek the gift of tongues, God prioritizes the gift of prophecy, because prophecy benefits believers and unbelievers more than tongues does (1 Corinthians 14:2-25). Paul gives the church a general guideline that everything must be done properly and in order, as seen in Paul's directive on the use of tongues in a worship service.

The next question from the Corinthians involves the future bodily resurrection of the dead. Paul first establishes that Christ had been raised bodily from the dead (1 Corinthians 15:1-28). Christ's resurrection is essential to the gospel and salvation, and historically attested to by many witnesses. The future bodily resurrection of believers is equally essential; otherwise, no reunion with Christ will ever take place (1 Corinthians 15:29-58). The believer's future bodily resurrection supplies an incentive to holy and missional living.

Last, Paul answers a question regarding a collection for a promised Jerusalem offering (1 Corinthians 16:1-4). Paul offers practical instruction about the Corinthians' contributions for the Jerusalem church, a contribution that acknowledges their spiritual indebtedness to the Jerusalem church.

Conclusion (1 Corinthians 16:5-24)

Paul concludes his letter by announcing his travel plans and giving general instructions regarding Timothy and Apollos. He also gives one last exhortation to the Corinthians to stand firm in the faith and do everything in love (1 Corinthians 16:13-14).

Living Out the Message of 1 Corinthians

First Corinthians has many key insights relevant to the contemporary church. First, it reminds us that church planting and discipleship are messy business. People saved out of a pagan culture bring with them many faulty ideas about life. Spiritual maturity comes with time. Discipling young converts requires patience and sometimes straight talk. In his introduction, Paul praises God for what the Lord has done among the Corinthians and especially for their spiritual giftedness. Yet at crucial points throughout the letter, Paul strongly rebukes their arrogance and haughtiness. Wise pastoral leadership knows when to exercise patience and when to speak forthrightly.

Second, the vastness of topics Paul handles helps us understand the necessity of training for those going into Christian ministry. Paul can speak clearly to so many issues because of his solid grounding in the Word of God. He also understands how to apply the Bible and its principles to daily living. Finally, even those not planning to go into church ministry need to know the Bible well. First Corinthians makes it clear that the ancient world had much in common with the present one. We have only one way to navigate the growing anti-Christian mindset in contemporary culture, whether it be sexual immorality, defining marriage, heretical teaching on the resurrection of Jesus, abuses of Christian freedom, or other issues touched on by Paul in this letter. We must know the Scriptures well.

8

2 Corinthians

The Glory and Heartache of Ministry

THE CHURCH AT CORINTH brought Paul both much joy—and much heartache. Eugene Peterson captures something of the situation when he writes, "The Corinthian Christians gave their founding pastor, Paul, more trouble than all of his other churches put together. No sooner did Paul get one problem straightened out in Corinth than three more appeared."[8]

The Big Picture

One might assume that Paul wrote 2 Corinthians shortly after 1 Corinthians, but a great deal transpired between the two letters. Putting together all of Paul's interactions with the Corinthians feels a little like assembling a puzzle. We know Paul wrote 1 Corinthians from Ephesus (1 Corinthians 16:8, 19). Timothy, who delivered the first letter, returned with news of significant Corinthian opposition to Paul. The apostle evidently made a "painful visit" to the church, not recorded in Acts. Second Corinthians implies such a visit, however (2 Corinthians 2:1; 12:14; 13:1-2). After Paul returned to Ephesus, he wrote a sorrowful letter urging the Corinthians to repent and to discipline the leader of the opposition (2 Corinthians 2:1-11; 7:8). Titus delivered that letter. Paul and Titus agreed to meet in Troas, although when Paul reached Troas before Titus did, the apostle traveled on to Macedonia, where the two reunited. Titus had good news (2 Corinthians 7:5-16). Much of the church had repented and eagerly awaited Paul's arrival, although a small but vocal minority still opposed him, apparently led by false apostles. This series of events prompted the writing of 2 Corinthians.

Paul wrote 2 Corinthians from Macedonia in AD 56, shortly before his third visit. He had three purposes in writing. First, he offered a word of encouragement to the reconciled majority (2 Corinthians 1–7). Second, he provided instructions for preparing a generous financial offering for the Jerusalem church (2 Corinthians 8–9). Third, he gave a word of rebuke and warning to the still-rebellious minority (2 Corinthians 10–13).

Outline

1. Introduction (2 Corinthians 1:1-11)

2. A Message of Reconciliation to the Loyal Majority (2 Corinthians 1:12–7:16)

3. Paul's Collection for the Judean Christians (2 Corinthians 8:1–9:15)

4. A Message to the Still-Rebellious Minority (2 Corinthians 10:1–13:10)

5. Conclusion (2 Corinthians 13:11-14)

Digging Into 2 Corinthians

Introduction (2 Corinthians 1:1-11)

In the same way that Sosthenes served with Paul when the apostle wrote 1 Corinthians, Timothy accompanied Paul during the writing of 2 Corinthians. Paul expresses his gratitude to God for the improved situation at Corinth (2 Corinthians 1:3-7) and for God's deliverance of him in Asia (2 Corinthians 1:8-11).

A Message of Reconciliation to the Loyal Majority (2 Corinthians 1:12-7:16)

In this section of the epistle, Paul addresses the now-loyal majority. Most of the congregation has lined up firmly behind him, with a smaller minority still following the false apostles. Paul will address them later in the letter.

We can divide Paul's account of his recent interactions with the Corinthians into five smaller units (2 Corinthians 1:12–2:13). First, Paul deals with accusations against his integrity (2 Corinthians 1:12-14). Some accused him of writing and saying one thing but meaning something else. He argues that he has conducted himself with holiness and single-mindedness, without deceit in what he said or did. Second, Paul explains the change in his travel plans (2 Corinthians 1:15–2:2). His opponents claim the abrupt change in his plans to visit Corinth indicates he cannot be trusted. Paul had to change his plans because of the turmoil in Corinth, which he describes as a "painful visit" (2 Corinthians 2:1). Third, Paul does not feel he can make yet another visit to Corinth, so he writes to them in anguish (2 Corinthians 2:3-4). When the situation changes sometime later, he will return. Fourth, he provides instruction on how to handle a matter of church discipline (2 Corinthians 2:5-11). Paul's reference to the majority reveals that most of the church stands solidly behind him. The offender mentioned in this passage is probably not the immoral man in 1 Corinthians 5, but the leader of the rebellion against Paul. Fifth, Paul expresses his anxiety as he waits to hear from Titus about his visit to Corinth (2 Corinthians 2:12-13). Although Paul had a great opportunity for evangelism in Troas, he traveled on to Macedonia, hoping to meet Titus there.

Then Paul sets forth the glory and suffering of Christian ministry (2 Corinthians 2:14–6:10). Despite the arduous nature of this ministry, the glory far exceeds the difficulties. Paul makes nine points concerning Christian ministry.

- Christian ministry is triumphant (2 Corinthians 2:14-16).
- Christian ministry is legitimate (2 Corinthians 3:1-3).
- Christian ministry is a new covenant task (2 Corinthians 3:4-18).
- Christian ministry is characterized by honesty and sincerity (2 Corinthians 4:1-6).
- Christian ministry perseveres even in difficulty (2 Corinthians 4:7-18).
- Christian ministry comes with an eternal reward (2 Corinthians 5:1-10).
- Christian ministry is motivated (2 Corinthians 5:11-17).
- Christian ministry brings reconciliation (2 Corinthians 5:18–6:2).
- Christian ministry is difficult (2 Corinthians 6:3-10).

Paul now appeals to the Corinthians for their continued acceptance and further affection (2 Corinthians 6:11–7:4). He expresses his heart for them and desires they do the same with him (2 Corinthians 6:11-13; 7:2-4). Some see 2 Corinthians 6:14–7:1 as a fragment from a "previous" letter because the verses seem out of place. These verses, however, are merely parenthetical, as Paul urges the Corinthians not to become involved with those who live in an ungodly way.

Paul hoped to meet Titus in Troas, but when he did not arrive, Paul pushed on to Macedonia (2 Corinthians 7:5-16). When they did meet, Titus brought good news. Most of the church had repented and felt eager to receive him, a good report that greatly relieved Paul.

Paul's Collection for the Judean Christians (2 Corinthians 8:1–9:15)

After Titus's report allows Paul to put his major concern behind him, the apostle turns his attention to the Jerusalem offering. In this portion of the letter, Paul exhorts the Corinthians to ready their generous offering by the time he arrives. Paul offers them four motivations to encourage their generosity: the example of the Macedonian churches (2 Corinthians 8:1-8), the generosity of Christ (2 Corinthians 8:9), their previous decision to give (2 Corinthians 8:10-12), and the existence of genuine need (2 Corinthians 8:13-15).

Paul urges the church to handle the collection arrangements with integrity (2 Corinthians 8:16–9:5). He sends Titus and two unnamed brethren to help in the completion of the offering. These verses provide an excellent reminder that Christians must handle all financial matters with openness and integrity.

In 2 Corinthians 9:6-15, Paul sets forth several principles of

Christian giving. First, we should give generously (2 Corinthians 9:6). Second, we should give voluntarily, without compulsion or reluctance. Why? God loves a cheerful giver (2 Corinthians 9:7). Third, generosity brings reward (2 Corinthians 9:8-11). Fourth, giving helps others (2 Corinthians 9:12). Fifth, and most important, generosity glorifies God (2 Corinthians 9:12-14).

A Message to the Still-Rebellious Minority (2 Corinthians 10:1-13:10)

Paul's tone changes at this point, a change so strong that some suggest the tone reveals it is part of another letter. We have no evidence, however, to support such a conclusion. This section opens with Paul's reply to false charges made against him by his opponents (2 Corinthians 10:1-18). They had accused Paul of cowardice (2 Corinthians 10:1-2, 9-12); that he employed worldly methods (2 Corinthians 10:3-6); that he was not a genuine apostle (2 Corinthians 10:7-8); and that Corinth lay outside his ministerial territory (2 Corinthians 10:13-18).

Though Paul feels hesitant to stoop to the level of his opponents, he decides he has no choice. He contrasts his apostleship with that of the false apostles (2 Corinthians 11:1–12:13). Paul feels deeply disappointed over the willingness of some Corinthians to receive these false teachers (2 Corinthians 11:1-6). Paul notes one significant difference between his apostleship and that of the false apostles: his refusal to accept financial support from the Corinthian church (2 Corinthians 11:7-15). He feels so strongly about the devious nature of these false apostles that he calls them servants of Satan (2 Corinthians 11:13-15).

In fact, Paul's apostleship is vastly superior to that of his opponents (2 Corinthians 11:16–12:13), as revealed by the fact he never took advantage of the Corinthians, as did the false apostles (2 Corinthians 11:16-21). He has a far superior pedigree (2 Corinthians 11:21-22). His sufferings indicate his superior qualifications as an apostle (2 Corinthians 11:23-33). The special revelations he has received also demonstrate his superiority (2 Corinthians 12:1-6). Even Paul's thorn in the flesh reflects his superiority to the false apostles (2 Corinthians 12:7-10). Finally, the miracles he performs far outshine anything done by the false apostles (2 Corinthians 12:11-13).

Paul declares his intention to visit Corinth a third time (2 Corinthians 12:14–13:10), when he will continue to refuse to take financial advantage of them (2 Corinthians 12:14-18). Although he has clear apprehensions about his upcoming visit (2 Corinthians 12:19-21), he will not fail to discipline those in opposition to him, if necessary (2 Corinthians 13:1-4). He calls on the Corinthians to examine themselves to make sure they are genuinely saved (2 Corinthians 13:5-10).

Conclusion (2 Corinthians 13:11-14)
Paul concludes his letter with personal greetings and with the grace, love, and fellowship that come from the Triune God: Father, Son, and Spirit.

Living Out the Message of 2 Corinthians
Second Corinthians reminds us that not everything in ministry goes well. Paul planted the church on his second missionary journey and spent eighteen months there discipling his spiritual converts. Yet, at some point, his relationship with the church deteriorated, a situation created by troubles of the church's own making. Some members felt too impressed by the false teachers. The Corinthians failed to compare the teachings of the false teachers to the teachings of Scripture and what Paul had taught them.

Although most of the church eventually repented of rebellion against Paul, he suffered deep anguish. We should never forget that Kingdom ministry is hard. Churches in Galatia and Corinth both caused Paul great heartache. God did not promise ministry would be easy, although we have an indescribable privilege to serve Jesus by serving his people.

Paul gives an impressive amount of space to the concept of giving, devoting two whole chapters to this important subject. Though Paul directs his teaching primarily to the Jerusalem offering, the principles remain relevant today. By giving generously, we express appropriate gratitude for Christ's sacrifice for his people (2 Corinthians 8:9).

9

Galatians

Justification by Faith

PAUL WROTE GALATIANS in the heat of battle, a fight for the hearts and souls of the churches of Galatia. The churches of Galatia had threatened to reject the truth of the gospel for a "different" gospel, which was not "the Good News" at all. Paul's distressed mindset reveals itself by how quickly he enters the argumentation portion of his letter. Paul normally speaks fondly of his readers in the opening sections and offers a prayer on their behalf. Instead, he declares his shock that the Galatians would so quickly turn away from the God who saved them.

The Big Picture

No one doubts Paul's authorship of Galatians, although some dispute the identity of the recipients. Some believe that Paul wrote to Galatians in the northern province of Asia Minor, while others believe he wrote to churches in the southern region of the Roman province of Galatia. Acts describes Paul planting churches in southern Galatia on his first missionary journey (Acts 13–14), but we do not know of any church planted by him in northern Galatia. Though no final determination on the matter may be possible, evidence favors the southern Galatia theory.

Some also dispute the date of the epistle. If Paul wrote to the Galatians after completing his first missionary journey, then a date of AD 48 seems probable. This early date would mean that Paul's two visits to Jerusalem, mentioned in Galatians 1 and 2, correspond to his initial visit to Jerusalem (Acts 9) and the famine relief visit (Acts 11). If the two Jerusalem visits mentioned in Galatians correspond to Paul's initial visit (Acts 9) and the Jerusalem conference visit (Acts 15), then he might have written the letter sometime later. Based upon Galatians' similarities to Romans, Paul may have

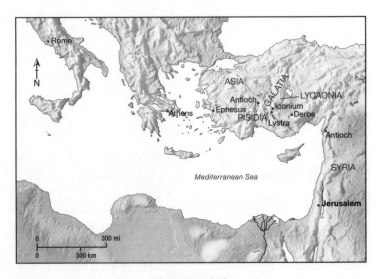

Cities in Galatia

written the former from Ephesus in approximately AD 53–54. Fortunately, the dating of the letter does not affect its interpretation.

Paul had a threefold purpose in writing Galatians: to defend his apostleship, defend the gospel, and explain how to live out the Christian life. Paul wrote the letter because the Galatians were in danger of abandoning the gospel. Paul wasted no time in getting to the heart of the issue (Galatians 1:6-10). We identify Paul's opponents as Judaizers who presented themselves as Jewish "Christians," but who taught a "different" gospel. They taught that Gentile believers must submit to the Mosaic law and that men must be circumcised.

Outline

1. Introduction (Galatians 1:1-10)

2. A Defense of Paul's Apostleship (Galatians 1:11–2:21)

3. A Defense of the Gospel (Galatians 3:1–4:31)

4. The Christian Life (Galatians 5:1–6:10)

5. Conclusion (Galatians 6:11-18)

Digging Into Galatians

Introduction (Galatians 1:1-10)

The opening verses of the letter contain the salutation (Galatians 1:1-5) and a statement of the circumstances that prompted the letter (Galatians 1:6-10). The seriousness of the circumstances is firmly established: the potential defection of the Galatians

(Galatians 1:6-7), the heresy of the Judaizers (Galatians 1:7-9), and the attack on Paul's integrity (Galatians 1:10).

A Defense of Paul's Apostleship (Galatians 1:11-2:21)

Paul begins by responding to the accusation that he has an inauthentic apostleship because the Jerusalem apostles never authorized him as a teacher of the Christian gospel (Galatians 1:11–2:21). He first affirms his independence from human authority (Galatians 1:11-24), contending that God himself had taught him and commissioned him as an apostle.

In Galatians 1:11-24, his argument unfolds in three steps: (1) His gospel came from God, not from humans; (2) his conversion and call came from God, not man; and (3) the events immediately following his conversion demonstrate that he did not come under the influence of the Jerusalem apostles. In fact, Paul did not return to Jerusalem until three years after his conversion.

Paul continues to defend his apostolic authority in Galatians 2:1-10, where he details another occasion in which he had contact with the Jerusalem apostles. While the previous section highlighted Paul's independence from the Jerusalem apostles, here he emphasizes their agreement with him on the matter of the gospel. Scholars debate whether this visit to Jerusalem refers to the famine relief visit in Acts 11:28-30 or the Jerusalem conference visit in Acts 15. Paul sets forth the occasion and circumstances for the visit (Galatians 2:1-2) and the circumstances surrounding Titus's involvement (Galatians 2:3-5). Though it is difficult to reconcile Paul's Jerusalem visits between Acts and Galatians, the visit appears to have more in common with the Jerusalem conference episode than the famine relief venture. Paul recounts the outcome of the meeting in 2:6-10. We can summarize the meeting in three thoughts: They imparted nothing to Paul (Galatians 2:6), they gave Paul and Barnabas the right hand of fellowship (Galatians 2:9), and they requested only that Paul and his associates remember the poor (Galatians 2:10).

We see a third part to Paul's argument concerning his independence from the Jerusalem apostles in his dramatic confrontation with Peter at Antioch (Galatians 2:11-21). When Peter first came to Antioch, he ate with uncircumcised Gentile Christians. When emissaries came from Jerusalem, however, he refused to eat with those same Gentile Christians. Peter felt intimidated by the circumcision group, and even Barnabas followed his poor example. Paul rebuked Peter to his face in a very dramatic moment (Galatians 2:14). The public nature of Peter's sin demanded a public rebuke. The issue at stake was the "truth of the gospel message." Verses 15-21 may summarize Paul's comments to Peter. The key verse three times mentions that justification cannot come by the works of the law (Galatians 2:16). Three times Paul likewise states the indispensability of faith.

A Defense of the Gospel (Galatians 3:1–4:31)

Having established his right to proclaim the gospel, Paul gets ready to argue for the truth of his gospel. The essence of Paul's gospel declares that justification comes through faith in Christ and that the works of the law contribute nothing to it. Paul develops his theme in this portion of the letter by setting forth a doctrinal argument.

Paul begins by pointing to the Galatians' own experience of receiving the Spirit by faith, not works (Galatians 3:1-5). Paul substantiates his point by declaring that Abraham's faith, not his works, justified him before God (Galatians 3:6-9). Those who seek salvation by obedience to the law are under a curse because no one can keep the law perfectly (Deuteronomy 27:26). God never intended the law as a means of salvation (Galatians 3:10-14). Paul refers to Habakkuk 2:4 to establish his point that the righteous live by faith. The law cannot take precedence over the covenant promise (Galatians 3:15-18), and God made the promise some 430 years before giving the law. The law was temporary until the coming of Christ (Galatians 3:21-24). The law and the promise do not contradict one another; they complement each other. Both have a role in the plan of God. The law cannot impart spiritual life, but is designed to cause people to become aware of their sin and grasp their need for salvation. The law is clearly inferior to the promise.

Paul then sets forth the standing of those who trust in the gospel (Galatians 3:25–4:11). We can break this section down into three smaller units. In Galatians 3:25-29, believers are children of God, one in Christ, and heirs according to the promise. In the next paragraph, Paul contrasts the essential difference between the Judaizers and Christianity (Galatians 4:1-7). Those who follow the Judaizers remain in bondage and do not know the freedom of the gospel. Those who believe in Paul's gospel are God's children and heirs. The presence of the Holy Spirit seals their adoption. In verses 8-11, Paul applies the results of his preceding argument to the Galatians. Before their conversion, the Galatians lived as pagans. When they came to faith in Christ, the Spirit set them free from bondage to idolatry and brought them into the knowledge of the one true and living God. The Galatians now are in danger of returning to bondage. Why would anyone return to a false gospel of legalism that cannot save?

To this point, the letter has a negative and argumentative tone. In Galatians 4:12, Paul changes to an attitude of entreaty and to a disposition of loving persuasion. He urges the Galatians to adopt his attitude toward the law. He reminds them of the devotion they once had for him and wonders why they have changed. He confesses that the Judaizers are courting them but calls their intentions evil. Paul closes the section with a fervent wish that he could be present with them so they could hear the gentle tone of his voice. The very personal paragraph reveals him pleading for the love and loyalty of his spiritual children.

Paul closes this section of the letter with an allegorical illustration drawn from biblical history (Galatians 4:21-31). He describes two branches of the Abrahamic family, one physical and the other spiritual. Those with a merely physical relationship to Abraham remain in bondage; those with a spiritual relationship to Abraham are truly free.

The Christian Life (Galatians 5:1-6:10)

The letter to the Galatians has focused so far on the means of a right relationship with God (Galatians 3–4); Paul now turns to a description of the life that should reflect that relationship (Galatians 5:1–6:10). Paul's discussion has highlighted the concept of freedom, and two perils threaten Christian freedom in Christ: legalism (Galatians 5:1-12) and license (Galatians 5:13-15). The former denies freedom; the latter perverts it. Paul encourages the Galatians to treasure their freedom from the yoke of the law and to refuse to be enslaved again (Galatians 5:1-12). The freedom to which Paul refers points back to the discussion of the preceding chapters, that is, freedom from the rigorous demands of the law as a means of gaining God's favor.

The question now becomes: How is this life possible, especially when considering the conflict within each believer between the flesh and the Spirit? Paul gives his answer in 5:16-26. Believers must "crucify" the flesh, a concept comparable to self-denial (Galatians 5:24), and they must walk/live by the Spirit (Galatians 5:16, 18, 25). Paul concludes with a warning against pride (Galatians 5:26).

Earlier in his letter, Paul mentions love as a characteristic of saving faith (Galatians 5:6), as a channel through which Christians serve one another (Galatians 5:13), as the fulfillment of the law (Galatians 5:14), and as a fruit of the Spirit (Galatians 5:22). Paul illustrates a life of love by including the restoration of those who fall into sin (Galatians 6:1), bearing one another's burdens (Galatians 6:2-5), supporting those who minister the Word (Galatians 6:6-8), and doing good to everyone (Galatians 6:9-10).

Conclusion (Galatians 6:11-18)

Paul concludes his letter with a summary of his major thoughts (Galatians 6:11-16), a personal appeal (Galatians 6:17), and a benediction (Galatians 6:18).

Living Out the Message of Galatians

Galatians makes it clear that faith alone justifies. No one can perfectly keep the law. In fact, God did not give the law for that purpose, but to reveal sin and our need for a Savior. We cannot live the Christian life without understanding the doctrine of justification, which lies at the heart of the gospel. To be justified is to be forgiven and counted righteous in Christ Jesus.

Paul's argument in the opening of the letter reveals the importance of his topic. Why else would he use such strong language as to pronounce a curse on those who preach another gospel? In fact, the gospel preached by the Judaizers was no gospel at all. The gospel is the Good News of salvation through faith in Christ, and the message of the Judaizers cannot save. Thus, Paul pronounces a curse because heaven and hell are at stake. To put one's faith in a gospel that cannot save has eternal consequences. Second, Paul pronounces a curse on the Judaizers because God's glory is at stake. God gets glory in the salvation of sinners. When people believe a lie instead of the truth, their belief fails to bring glory to God. Paul opens his letter with such passion because eternal, infinite things are at stake.

Paul's testimony in Galatians 1:11-24 demonstrates God's power to change the hardest and worst of sinners. Paul had been a violent persecutor of the church. While Paul was on his way to Damascus to arrest believers in Christ, Christ met him. We see God's power both in Paul's conversion and in his dramatic change in attitude toward Christ and his people. If God can save Paul, then he can save even the hardest among us. Do not despair, imagining that those for whom you pray have no hope. Remember God's gracious work in the hardened heart of Paul and take courage!

Finally, those who believe the gospel must demonstrate their faith by living out the gospel. Gospel living rejects both legalism and libertinism. Gospel living crucifies the flesh with its passions and desires, by the power of the Spirit. Believers manifest the fruit of the Spirit in their interactions with others and by bearing one another's burdens. The doctrine of justification by faith has practical implications for the daily lives of each of Christ's followers.

10

Ephesians

God's Glory in the Church

PAUL'S LETTERS to the Ephesians, Philippians, Colossians, and Philemon are known as his Prison Epistles (Ephesians 3:1; 4:1; 6:20; Philippians 1:7, 13, 17; Colossians 4:3, 10, 18; Philemon 1:1). Scholars generally believe Paul wrote them during his first Roman imprisonment between AD 60 and 62 (Acts 25:11-12; 28:30-31), but reading them makes it hard to imagine that Paul had been incarcerated for several years. Ephesians and Colossians extol the greatness of Christ, and many think these two letters most clearly present Paul's cosmic Christology (more on this later). Though Paul may have been under house arrest for several years, his spiritual life flourished. Rather than diminishing Paul's view of God's greatness, imprisonment expanded it.

The Big Picture

Paul started the church at Ephesus on his third missionary journey and spent approximately three years there (Acts 19:1-41). Paul had such an effective ministry in Ephesus that the gospel spread throughout Asia during those years (Acts 19:10). Paul spent more time in Ephesus than in any other city where he planted a church.

Ephesus, one of the largest cities in the Roman empire, also served as the capital of the Roman province of Asia (modern-day Turkey). The city had both commercial and religious importance. Ephesus, a center for emperor worship, overflowed with many temples, the most important of which was the temple of Artemis (Diana). Her temple was known as one of the seven wonders of the ancient world (Acts 19:23-34).

To appreciate Ephesians fully, we must understand the role played in the city by the magical arts. While magic and related practices were performed throughout the empire, they played an especially important role in Ephesus. We see the significance of the magical arts in Luke's description of Paul's ministry there (Acts 19:11-20). The citizens of Ephesus needed no convincing about an unseen world of spiritual beings. Though the church at Ephesus was planted in a "hard place," it thrived under Paul's leadership. Many of those who heard the letter read in their congregational gatherings had been won to Christ during Paul's ministry (AD 52–55).

Though some scholars doubt Paul's authorship of the letter, a strong case can be made for its authenticity. The letter itself claims to be written by Paul (Ephesians 1:1; 3:1), and nothing in it contradicts his authorship. The early church writers never called Paul's authorship into question. Later critics point to perceived differences in vocabulary, writing style, and theology from Paul's undisputed letters, such as Romans and Galatians, but these differences are not nearly as significant as sometimes suggested. Some scholars point to similar content in Colossians as evidence of other authorship, but these differences can be explained easily by noting that Paul addresses common dangers.

Paul does not state the specific occasion and purpose that prompted him to write this letter. The similarities to Colossians suggest a similar concern for the church at Ephesus. The two books differ in that while the church at Colossae was already under attack from heretical teaching, the church at Ephesus did not yet face that threat. Paul's major theme in Ephesians is God's glory in the church. The letter uses several images to describe the church (body, bride, temple, and family). Paul sends the letter by Tychicus, who also delivered Paul's letter to Colossae (Ephesians 6:21; Colossians 4:9). Paul likely wrote the book in his first Roman imprisonment, probably around AD 61.

Finally, we need to consider the authenticity of the words "in Ephesus" (Ephesians 1:1). Some of the best and oldest manuscripts lack these words. Many scholars believe Ephesians originally was a circular letter, written to churches in Asia. That is certainly possible, but even if it's true, this would not affect the letter's interpretation. In that case, however, it would be the only circular letter written by Paul in the New Testament. In addition, the words "at Ephesus" appear in the majority of manuscripts. Therefore, the authenticity of those words is slightly favored.

Before examining the content of the letter, it may help to recognize some important themes and topics it addresses. First, Ephesians uses the phrase "in the heavenly realms" five times (Ephesians 1:3, 20; 2:6; 3:10; 6:12); the phrase appears nowhere else in the Bible. Each reference adds some nuance to our understanding. Second, the word "love" (*agape*) appears more often in Ephesians than in any other New Testament book, with the exceptions of 1 Corinthians and 1 John. Third, pay special attention to the various references and images used for the church. The church is essential to God's plan. Fourth, Paul often reminds the Ephesians of their spiritual condition before they met Christ. These reminders motivate believers to love Jesus more fully and follow him more faithfully.

Outline

We can break down the letter into two equal parts. The first half lays a doctrinal foundation, while the second half focuses on Christian living. As we have seen in other Pauline writings, doctrine provides the foundation for holy living.

1. Salutation (Ephesians 1:1-2)

2. Doctrinal Foundation (Ephesians 1:3–3:21)
    a. What God has done for us in Christ (Ephesians 1:3-23)
    b. What God has done in us in Christ (Ephesians 2:1-10)
    c. What God has done between us in Christ (Ephesians 2:11–3:21)

3. Practical Application (Ephesians 4:1–6:20)
    a. The church's unity and growth (Ephesians 4:1-16)
    b. The believer's walk in Christ (Ephesians 4:17–6:9)
    c. The believer's warfare (Ephesians 6:10-20)

4. Conclusion (Ephesians 6:21-24)

Digging Into Ephesians

Salutation (Ephesians 1:1-2)

These verses give the traditional Pauline introduction, identifying the writer and intended recipients, as well as extending blessings of grace and peace.

Doctrinal Foundation (Ephesians 1:3-3:21)

The opening section contains one of the most beautiful Trinitarian passages in the Bible (Ephesians 1:3-14). Believers are chosen by the Father (Ephesians 1:3-6), redeemed by the blood of the Son (Ephesians 1:7-12), and sealed by the Spirit (Ephesians 1:13-14). God has not withheld any spiritual blessing from those in Christ (Ephesians 1:3). The blessings found in the passage include election to holiness (Ephesians 1:4); adoption into God's family (Ephesians 1:5); redemption and forgiveness (Ephesians 1:7); wisdom and understanding to comprehend God's cosmic plan (Ephesians 1:8); the believer's inheritance (Ephesians 1:13); and the sealing of believers by the Holy Spirit (Ephesians 1:14). All of this accrues to the praise of God's glorious grace (Ephesians 1:6, 12, 14).

Paul turns from praise to prayer as he intercedes for the church (Ephesians 1:15-23). He feels motivated to pray and give thanks to God for them because of their faith in Jesus and love for God's people. Paul asks that they come to know God better—that God would open the eyes of their hearts to know the hope of God's calling, the glory of God's inheritance in the saints, and the greatness of God's power. The greatness of God's power is manifested by Jesus' resurrection, exaltation, universal dominion, and headship over the church. Knowing that their Savior is Lord over all would bring great comfort to a people who once feared the power of unseen spiritual forces.

In chapter 2, Paul focuses further on the salvation his readers have experienced in Christ (Ephesians 2:1-10). Before salvation, they were spiritually dead, spiritually enslaved (to the world, Satan, and the flesh), and spiritually condemned (Ephesians 2:1-3). But God, rich in mercy, great in love, and incomparably gracious, saved them, not based on anything they had done (Ephesians 2:4-10). God made them alive together with Christ, raised them up with

Christ, and seated them with Christ in the heavenly places. People receive this salvation by faith. Those who have been saved by grace demonstrate their salvation by performing good works, which God has prepared in advance for them to do.

God reconciles Jews and Gentiles to himself and to one another (Ephesians 2:11-22). The law no longer separates Jews and Gentiles; instead, they have been made one and equally share in the benefits of the gospel. They make up one new humanity, a Kingdom family, a temple indwelt by God's Spirit, held together by the cornerstone, Jesus Christ.

Paul next explains his ministry as apostle to the Gentiles (Ephesians 3:1-13). He describes how God has entrusted him with a *mystery*: God always intended for Gentile believers to share in the blessings of the gospel. God also entrusted Paul with a *ministry* to proclaim to the Gentiles the gospel message (Ephesians 3:7-13). The doctrinal section concludes with a second magnificent prayer (Ephesians 3:14-21) that focuses on three major requests. First, that the Ephesians would be strengthened with power in their inner person. Second, that they would comprehend the incomprehensible nature of God's love for them. Third, that they would be filled with all the fullness of God. If all these things sound like too much to ask, remember that God can do much more—far more than anyone can think or imagine, and all to the glory of God.

Practical Application (Ephesians 4:1-6:20)

The doctrinal section ends with "Amen," while the practical section begins with "Therefore." In the second half of the letter, Paul explains how doctrine shapes the Christian life. Paul begins by focusing on the corporate nature of Christianity. He explains that Christian character and doctrine are foundational for church unity

(Ephesians 4:1-6). Paul moves from the unity of the church to her diversity and growth (both spiritually and numerically; Ephesians 4:7-16). The diversity of gifts within the church enables believers to build up one another in the faith for the spiritual maturity of all. Every Christian has a spiritual gift, and every believer is important to the life and health of the church.

Paul then admonishes believers to live changed lives (Ephesians 4:17–6:9). They should no longer live and think as non-Christians do (Ephesians 4:17-19), but rather live transformed lives based on truth and evidenced by holiness (Ephesians 4:20-25). Furthermore, Paul wants his readers to emulate God's love (Ephesians 5:1-2) and purity (Ephesians 5:3-14). Immorality characterized the ancient world (and continues to do so in our modern one). The children of light should resist sexual immorality in all its forms.

Paul next turns to the walk of the wise (Ephesians 5:15-20). Those who live wisely seek to discern God's will, redeem the time, and seek to continually be filled with the Spirit. Spirit-filled believers demonstrate the Spirit's work in their lives by speaking encouragingly to one another, singing joyfully to God, giving thanks for God's good gifts, and submitting to one another.

Submission to the Spirit radically changes believers' lives and relationships, especially their family relationships, as by God's power they live out their God-given roles (Ephesians 5:21–6:4). Wives submit to their husbands, husbands sacrificially love their wives as Christ loved the church, and children obey and honor their parents. The work of the Spirit in the life of a Christian family generates all these attitudes and actions. In addition, the Spirit transforms how servants and masters relate to one another (Ephesians 6:5-9).

Spirit-filled believers should not presume any exemption from enemy attacks. Paul addresses the important topic of the believer's warfare (Ephesians 6:10-20).[9] Already he has warned his readers not to give the devil a foothold (Ephesians 4:26-27). Now he gives two primary commands: "Be strong in the Lord" (Ephesians 6:10), and "Put on all of God's armor" (Ephesians 6:11). Both the spiritual strength and the armor needed for spiritual combat come from God.

Most spiritual warfare requires resisting the enemy's attack (temptation). The church has a cunning, wicked, powerful, and persistent enemy (Ephesians 6:11-12). Observe Paul's emphasis on *standing firm* and *standing your ground* (Ephesians 6:11, 13-14). This repeated emphasis teaches that the enemy works to make believers fall into sin. No believer should underestimate the enemy—or his power and craftiness. The word translated "fighting" conveys the idea of hand-to-hand combat, much like a wrestling match. God has provided believers with three offensive weapons: gospel boots, the sword of the Spirit (Word of God), and prayer. When believers share the gospel, they invade enemy territory with a message that sets captives free. If the Word is to be used effectively in spiritual combat, it must be known, believed, and obeyed. Remember how effectively Jesus used the sword of the Spirit in his wilderness battle with the devil (Luke 4:1-13)? One of the believer's most powerful weapons may be intercessory prayer. Believers should "Pray in the Spirit at all times and on every occasion" (Ephesians 6:18). Christians must stay alert and not give up on prayer. Much of the believer's prayer life should include intercession.

Conclusion (Ephesians 6:21-24)

Paul commends his helper and courier, Tychicus. He closes the letter as he opened it: with blessings of peace and grace.

Living Out the Message of Ephesians

Paul's teaching about Jesus Christ is one of the most important truths to grasp in Ephesians. Read through the opening section and notice all the references to Jesus (Ephesians 1:3-14). *All* of God's blessings come to believers because of their relationship to Jesus Christ. The Savior the church loves and serves has been raised from the dead and exalted to God's right hand (Ephesians 1:19-23). All things will one day bow to Jesus as Lord (Ephesians 1:9-10).

Ephesians has much to teach about the church, also called a Kingdom, a family, and a temple (Ephesians 2:19-22). The church is one new man, made up of believing Jews and Gentiles (Ephesians 2:14-15). The church is the bride of Christ, for which he laid down his life (Ephesians 5:25-27, 29, 32). God greatly glorifies himself through the church (Ephesians 3:21) and reveals his wisdom to rulers and authorities in heavenly places through it (Ephesians 3:10). In an age when many depreciate the church and see it as an inconvenience to their busy schedules, Christ's body remains at the center of God's love. It may not be too strong to say that one cannot fully love God without loving his bride, the church.

The longest passage on Christian marriage in the New Testament is found in Ephesians 5:22-33. Spirit-filled husbands should sacrificially love their wives as Christ loves the church. Christian husbands should serve their wives and families as servant leaders. Wives should lovingly respect their husbands and follow their husband's leadership in the home. God's plan calls for the relationship between a husband and wife to mirror the glorious relationship between Christ and his church.

Finally, we must not forget the importance of spiritual warfare discussed throughout the letter, culminating in the most significant passage in the Bible on the topic (Ephesians 6:10-20). The Christian life is a life of warfare. Christians, however, have nothing to fear. Believers serve their victorious Savior, empowered by his Spirit and clothed in the armor that God provides. One of the most important battles Christians can fight is in intercessory prayer, highlighted not only in Ephesians 6:18-20, but in the two powerful prayers Paul prayed for the Ephesian church. These Spirit-inspired prayers came from God through the pen of Paul. When you do not know what to pray for others, pray these two prayers (Ephesians 1:15-23; 3:14-21).

11

Philippians

Rejoice in the Lord

PAUL WROTE PHILIPPIANS from prison. Many Christians regard Philippians as their favorite book in the Bible. One reason for its popularity is its frequent repetition of the word "joy." Few, however, realize that when Paul wrote this letter, he had been incarcerated for several years. Clearly, Paul grounded his joy in Christ and not in his circumstances.

The Big Picture

Paul planted the church at Philippi on his second missionary journey (Acts 16:11-40). Despite the difficulty of his work, Paul left behind a solid church. Few question the authorship of Philippians. Paul wrote the book during his first Roman imprisonment, about AD 62. He likely penned the letter not long before his release. The return of Epaphroditus to the church—Epaphroditus served as the Philippians' emissary to Paul—occasioned the writing of the letter.

Paul had at least five purposes for writing the letter. First, he desired to encourage the church to seek unity through humility (Philippians 2:1-11). Readers of Philippians often think this church had no outstanding issues, but the letter indicates some serious church divisions. Second, Paul wanted to report to the church his situation and the progress of the gospel (Philippians 1:12-17). Despite Paul's incarceration, the gospel went out widely. Third, the apostle intended to commend Timothy and Epaphroditus to the church (Philippians 2:19-30). These two men demonstrated the humility of Jesus Christ, and the church should follow their example. Fourth, Paul warns the church against false teaching (Philippians 3:1-21). Though the Philippians were in danger from Judaizers and their message of legalism, they also were in danger of libertinism at the other extreme. Fifth, Paul wrote to express his deep gratitude for their generous financial assistance (Philippians 4:10-20). On more than one occasion, this church sent financial help to Paul and his companions.

Outline

1. Salutation, Thanksgiving, and Prayer (Philippians 1:1-11)

2. An Account of Paul's Circumstances (Philippians 1:12-26)

3. Entreaties to the Philippians (Philippians 1:27–2:18)

4. Plans for Timothy and Epaphroditus (Philippians 2:19-30)

5. Warning concerning Spiritual Dangers (Philippians 3:1-21)

6. General Exhortations (Philippians 4:1-9)

7. Gratitude for the Philippians' Support (Philippians 4:10-20)

8. Conclusion (Philippians 4:21-23)

Digging Into Philippians

Salutation, Thanksgiving, and Prayer (Philippians 1:1-11)

Paul's opening lines imply the church was struggling with unity. Rather than identifying himself as an apostle, Paul identifies himself and Timothy as "slaves of Christ Jesus." In chapter 2, he refers to Jesus using the word "slave" (Philippians 2:7). Paul specifically mentions "church leaders and deacons" among the holy ones he addresses, which seems odd, almost as if some might not identify them by this term. Paul's comments in 2:1-4 and his reference to two ladies struggling with one another (Philippians 4:2) suggest the church needed to demonstrate humility and unity. Paul's prayer of gratitude to God for the church reflects the close relationship he had with the believers there (Philippians 1:3-11).

An Account of Paul's Circumstances (Philippians 1:12-26)

As Paul describes his circumstances, he demonstrates deep confidence in God's providence. He understands that God has used everything that happened to him (from his arrest in Jerusalem to his imprisonment in Rome) to advance the gospel. Paul's incarceration has allowed him to share the Good News with his Roman

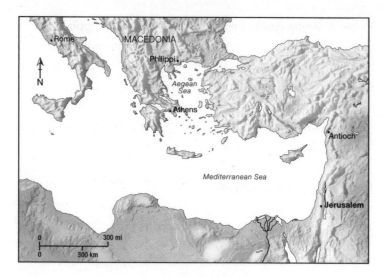

Location of Philippi

guards. Even the Roman Christians have begun sharing the Good News more boldly because of Paul's imprisonment.

Entreaties to the Philippians (Philippians 1:27–2:18)

Paul makes several entreaties to his readers. He wants them to stand firm in one spirit despite opposition (Philippians 1:27-28). Next, Paul turns his attention to the church's unity (Philippians 2:1-11). Looking to Jesus as the best example to emulate, they should consider one another better than themselves and look out for one another's interests rather than just their own concerns (Philippians 2:5-11). Philippians 2:5-11 is often called "the Christ hymn." Whether Paul wrote it or simply incorporated it into his letter, the hymn fits perfectly in this context. If Jesus willingly died for them, how could they not look out for the best interests of others? Paul rounds out this section by appealing to his readers for their obedience (Philippians 2:12-18). Complaining and arguing demonstrate a lack of concern for others.

Plans for Timothy and Epaphroditus (Philippians 2:19-30)

Paul's commendation of Timothy and Epaphroditus demonstrates how they reflect his admonition to consider others before oneself. Paul seems to feel a special need to explain to the Philippians why he is sending Epaphroditus back. He wants them to understand that Epaphroditus has faithfully fulfilled the mission for which the church had sent him, and they should receive him well.

Warning concerning Spiritual Dangers (Philippians 3:1-21)

The church faced two theological dangers: legalism and libertinism. Paul spends more time confronting the former, as propagated by Judaizers (Philippians 3:1-16), than he does the latter. Within this section he warns against the danger of religious pride based upon personal achievements (Philippians 3:4-6). Every religious accomplishment counts as nothing when compared to the value of knowing Christ Jesus in his death and resurrection (Philippians 3:7-11). The opposite trap to legalism, a libertine lifestyle, worships a god of appetite (Philippians 3:17-21)—an approach to living unworthy of citizens of heaven.

General Exhortations (Philippians 4:1-9)

Paul makes three final appeals to the Philippians: steadfastness, unity, and living with joy and peace in a turbulent world. Paul urges Euodia and Syntyche to work together. The differences between the two ladies must not have been doctrinal, or Paul would have addressed the matter.

Gratitude for the Philippians' Support (Philippians 4:10-20)

He begins to wrap up his letter with a heartfelt expression of gratitude for the church's generosity to him (Philippians 4:10-20). Within this section, he explains the secret of contentment: being satisfied in Jesus, whether one has much or little. Contentment grows best in the soil of gratitude. These verses remind us that Paul's apostleship involved much hardship.

Conclusion (Philippians 4:21-23)
Paul concludes his letter with a warm greeting. He mentions those of Caesar's household, implying that some of Nero's own servants follow Jesus. Yes, the gospel can reach even the darkest of places.

Living Out the Message of Philippians
Joy is a major theme in Philippians. Paul's joy came from Christ and not out of his circumstances. Despite several years of incarceration, he still rejoiced in the Lord. When we rejoice in the Lord, we focus on everything God has done for us, his children in Christ, rather than allowing our circumstances to determine our level of joy. Paul focused on the person and work of Christ and the salvation he secured. Therefore, we must take our eyes off ourselves and focus them directly on Jesus.

The Christ hymn in Philippians 2:5-11 is one of the great Christological passages in the New Testament. These verses demonstrate what humility and considering others better than oneself looks like. But they do more than highlight Jesus as an example of selflessness. In the first half of the hymn, Jesus is the subject of the verbs. In other words, verses 5-8 demonstrate what Jesus did. The main thought holds that he did not use his equality with God to his own advantage, but instead humbled himself by becoming a slave, taking on flesh and blood (becoming a human being), and obeying God by dying like a common criminal on a cross. The second half of the hymn focuses on what God did for Jesus because of his Son's humble actions. God exalted him to the highest place and gave him the name above all names. At the name of Jesus, every tongue will confess that Jesus Christ is Lord, to the glory of God!

The final passage explains how Paul could experience joy and peace in all of life's circumstances (Philippians 4:4-9). Paul exhorts the Philippians to "be full of joy in the Lord." He doesn't command them to rejoice in their circumstances, but to glory in the person and work of Christ on their behalf. They must show consideration to one another, keeping in mind the nearness of the Lord's coming. Difficult circumstances have a way of making us harsh and unkind, so it takes determination to consider the well-being of others. Prayer defeats worry. Believers should pray about everything, no matter how big or small the issue. When a person makes prayer their first choice and not their last hope, then God's peace stands as a guard, protecting their heart and mind. In addition, believers must take every thought captive, meditating on whatever is pure and godly and rejecting the impure and ungodly. Paul promises that when we do this, the God of peace will be with us.

12

Colossians

The Supremacy of Christ

WHO IS JESUS? The book of Colossians answers that question, loud and clear. Consider one sample of what Paul teaches in Colossians about Jesus:

> Christ is the visible image of the invisible God.
>> He existed before anything was created and is supreme
>>> over all creation,
> for through him God created everything
>> in the heavenly realms and on earth.
> He made the things we can see
>> and the things we can't see—
> such as thrones, kingdoms, rulers, and authorities in the
>> unseen world.

> Everything was created through him and for him.
> He existed before anything else,
>> and he holds all creation together.

COLOSSIANS 1:15-17

And think of it: This passage declares *only a little* of what Paul says about Jesus in this book! But why the focus on Christ's supremacy? A heresy endangered the church by depreciating the significance of Jesus. R. C. Lucas perfectly captures the sense of the danger in Colossae when he writes,

> If Christ's is the power which sustains the whole universe from remote beginnings to its final goal . . . , is it reasonable to doubt his power to sustain the individual believer from conversion to glory? Put in this way it would, of course, be absurd, even monstrous, to deny the adequacy of Christ. But, as we shall see, something like that was happening [in Colossae].[10]

The Big Picture

Colossians is one of Paul's Prison Epistles. Although scholars debate Paul's authorship. the letter claims to be written by Paul (Colossians 1:1, 23; 4:18), and the early church writers never disputed Paul's authorship. Those who doubt that Paul wrote the book point to many of the same issues associated with their doubts concerning Paul's authorship of Ephesians. They suggest the vocabulary and style of writing are unlike Paul's undisputed letters (i.e., Romans, Galatians, 1 Corinthians).

The differences in vocabulary and style from Paul's undisputed letters, however, almost certainly have to do with differences in the issues Paul addresses. Those who dispute Paul's authorship also point to theological differences between Colossians and Paul's undisputed letters. These theological differences certainly result from addressing different problems in the churches. Those who deny Paul's authorship also point to its similarities to Ephesians, but these similarities can be explained easily by the fact that Paul addresses comparable topics. No overwhelming reason exists to deny Pauline authorship of Colossians. Paul wrote Colossians from Rome during his first imprisonment there (Colossians 4:3, 10, 18), probably in AD 61.

Colossae sat in the Lycus River Valley, approximately 100 miles east of Ephesus. By Paul's day, the formerly wealthy and populous Colossae had declined significantly. Paul's concern for the church reminds us that God loves every church, regardless of its setting. The letter also provides a striking reminder that big problems can happen anywhere, even in small places.

A man named Epaphras, and not Paul himself, apparently founded the church during Paul's ministry at Ephesus. Epaphras reported to Paul the danger of an encroaching heresy. "The Colossian heresy" combined Christianity with Jewish legalism and pagan philosophy to form a syncretistic error. The false teachers taught that faith in Jesus Christ was not enough. Full salvation came through knowledge gained by spiritual illumination. In addition, adherents had to follow Jewish dietary laws, celebrate Jewish festivals, practice asceticism, and engage in the worship of angels (Colossians 2:16-18). Paul's letter reminds us again of the importance of doctrinal fidelity.

Paul writes to the Colossians after hearing Epaphras's report of the heresy diminishing the significance of Jesus Christ. Paul sets out to demonstrate the supremacy and sufficiency of Jesus over and against this heretical teaching. Paul spends little time debating his opponents point-by-point, but rather, focuses his attention on teaching the Colossians the truth. The main point of Colossians is the supremacy of Christ and how Christ meets *all* the spiritual needs of his people.

Outline

1. Introduction (Colossians 1:1-14)

2. The Supremacy of Christ (Colossians 1:15-23)

3. Paul's Ministry (Colossians 1:24–2:7)

4. The Dangerous Heresy Threatening the Church (Colossians 2:8-23)

5. Living the Christian Life (Colossians 3:1–4:6)

6. Final Instructions and Greetings (Colossians 4:7-18)

Digging Into Colossians

Introduction (Colossians 1:1-14)
Paul begins the letter in his typical fashion by introducing himself and addressing his readers (Colossians 1:1-2). Paul expresses gratitude to God for the spiritual growth of the Colossians, the progress of the gospel, and the ministry of Epaphras (Colossians 1:3-8). Paul prays that they will have a full understanding of the will of God, so that they might live in a way worthy of God (Colossians 1:9-14). Spiritual knowledge is meant to transform how believers live. They should desire to please the Lord in all things. Paul explains that this kind of life bears spiritual fruit,

fosters an intimate knowledge of God, develops strength to bear up under difficult circumstances, and demonstrates patience with difficult people. Paul concludes his prayer by thanking God for the blessings of salvation (Colossians 1:12-14).

The Supremacy of Christ (Colossians 1:15-23)

Thematically, the letter shifts focus from the believer's blessings in Christ to the supremacy of Christ. Paul begins a subtle attack on the heresy threatening the church, which taught a defective Christology. In one of the most important Christological passages in the New Testament, Paul declares that Jesus Christ is Lord of creation and Lord of the church (Colossians 1:15-23).

Because of its rhythmic structure, many consider Colossians 1:15-20 to be an ancient hymn that Paul incorporated into his letter. More likely, however, the words are original to Paul. Jesus is "the visible image of the invisible God" (Colossians 1:15). Paul means that Jesus Christ is eternal God. Jesus is Lord of creation because he created it (Colossians 1:15-17). Creation owes its unity, meaning, and existence to him, and he created it for his own glory.

Jesus is also Lord over the church (Colossians 1:18). Paul bases his assertion of Christ's lordship on two truths. First, all the fullness of God dwells in Christ (Colossians 1:19). To say "God in all his fullness was pleased to live in Christ" means that Christ is God. Second, Christ's work on the cross reconciles believers to God (Colossians 1:20-23). Considering who Christ is and what he has accomplished, they must continue to trust in him and not become sidetracked by heretical teachers (Colossians 1:23).

Paul's Ministry (Colossians 1:24-2:7)

Since Paul did not plant the church at Colossae, he felt compelled to explain his ministry. God himself commissioned the apostle's ministry (Colossians 1:25), which involves his suffering for the church. In saying "I am participating in the sufferings of Christ" (Colossians 1:24), Paul indicates that just as Christ suffered, so his followers will suffer. When believers suffer for Christ, in some sense he suffers with them (Acts 9:4-5; 2 Corinthians 1:5; Philippians 3:10).

Paul's ministry includes preaching (Colossians 1:25-29). The content of his preaching centers on the Good News, which he describes as a "secret." In the New Testament, a "secret" refers to that which God has hidden, something known only by God until God chooses to reveal it. Paul aims in his preaching "to present them to God, perfect in their relationship to Christ" (Colossians 1:28).

Third, in his ministry, Paul agonizes for "his" churches in prayer (Colossians 2:1-3). Prayer means war. Throughout his letters, Paul prays consistently for fellow believers. Paul wants the church to feel encouraged and, most importantly, to know Christ, for "in him lie hidden all the treasures of wisdom and knowledge" (Colossians 2:3).

The Dangerous Heresy Threatening the Church (Colossians 2:8-23)

Paul next dissects the heresy invading the Colossian church. First, he warns the Colossians concerning the danger of false philosophies, which take people prisoner (Colossians 2:8-15). The term "philosophy" may be applied to theories about religion, the world, and the meaning of life. Paul does not condemn all philosophical thought, but only that which originates from "human thinking and from the spiritual powers of this world, rather than from Christ" (Colossians 2:8). In contrast to this false philosophy, the fullness of God dwells in Christ and makes believers complete in him (Colossians 2:9-14). In Christ, the Colossian Christians have the true circumcision and genuine forgiveness of sin, and they share in Christ's victory over spiritual powers. Their union with Christ meets their every spiritual need.

Paul next turns to the dangers of legalism, angel worship, and asceticism (Colossians 2:16-23). Some of these elements reveal the "Jewish flavor" of the Colossian heresy. The reference to food and drink refers to Jewish food laws, the special days to Jewish festivals, and the Sabbath to the rules governing Sabbath observance. The food laws, festivals, and Sabbath observance in the Old Testament all pointed toward Jesus, but now in Christ these shadows have been fulfilled. The need for them no longer exists.

First-century Jewish people commonly engaged in angel worship. The author of Hebrews also dealt with this issue (Hebrews 1:5-14). Though many contemporary forms of spirituality give angels a lofty place in their religious practices, God created angels to worship and serve him, not to be worshiped. The Colossian heretics may have given angels a prominent role in their teaching, suggesting angels mediated visions and revelations from God to them.

Finally, Paul addresses the heresy of asceticism. Although asceticism—practicing extreme forms of self-denial—seems spiritual, it falsely follows man-made rules and regulations. These rules and regulations come from diabolical spiritual powers, rather than from God's Word. Asceticism cannot deal with the issues of the heart, but focuses merely on external standards. Though this sort of spirituality has the appearance of wisdom, Paul argues that it does not come from God and cannot fulfill its promises. Only through Christ does one find both victory over the indulgences of the flesh and true devotion to God.

Living the Christian Life (Colossians 3:1-4:6)

Because of the Colossians' union with Christ, Paul urges them to "set [their] sights on the realities of heaven" (Colossians 3:1) and "think about the things of heaven" (Colossians 3:2). Paul exhorts his readers to center their lives on Christ (Colossians 3:3-4). Things of the earth might include centering one's thoughts on material wealth, worldly power, or earthly pleasures. Christians must not make these things a life goal or the substance of their thoughts. Believers seek the things that truly matter because Christians have been resurrected to newness of life with Christ. The believers' true lives are hidden with Christ in God.

Paul now begins to explain what a life that sets its sights on heaven looks like. First, it deals seriously with sin by putting it to death (Colossians 3:5-11) and by putting on the virtues of the new life in Christ (Colossians 3:12-17). Love, peace, and the indwelling of Christ's Word characterize the new life. Everything should be done for the glory of Christ (Colossians 3:17).

One of the most difficult places to live out these virtues is within the confines of one's family (Colossians 3:18–4:1). We often let down our spiritual guards in the home, but especially in a believer's family, holiness must be lived out. Husbands should love their wives and treat them with great kindness. Wives should joyfully submit to their husband's leadership. Children must honor and obey their parents. Slaves should serve their masters for God's glory, and masters must treat their slaves in a way that honors God.

Paul encourages his readers to devote themselves to prayer (Colossians 4:2-3). He asks them to pray for him. Paul does not ask them to pray for his release from prison, but that he might declare the Good News with clarity and boldness. He encourages the Colossians to take advantage of every opportunity to spread the gospel (Colossians 4:5-6).

Final Instructions and Greetings (Colossians 4:7-18)

Paul has a rather lengthy conclusion in which he includes some final instructions and greetings. He asks them to remember his imprisonment. Paul writes the letter's final words with his own hand.

Living Out the Message of Colossians

Colossians focuses on the supremacy of Christ. The book puts Paul's cosmic Christology on full display. Paul has stunning things to say about Jesus Christ: Jesus is the image of the invisible God; Jesus is the creator and sustainer of the universe; Jesus is both the redeemer and head of the church; in Jesus are hidden all the treasures of wisdom and knowledge; in Jesus dwells all the fullness of God; every believer is complete in Jesus; Jesus defeated every demonic power at the cross. What Paul says about Jesus should cause the church to sing more loudly, give more generously, and serve him more faithfully.

13

1 Thessalonians

Future Hope in a Hostile World

FIRST THESSALONIANS GIVES US a glimpse of a first-century church plant. The letter provides a beautiful picture of Paul's discipleship of a young, fledgling congregation. Paul's Thessalonian letters are known as his eschatological epistles because of the amount of space he devotes in them to Christ's second coming.

The Big Picture

Paul may have written 1 Thessalonians before any of his other New Testament letters (depending on the date of Galatians). Scholars widely accept Pauline authorship. Paul started the church on his second missionary journey (Acts 17:1-9). Thessalonica, the capital of the Roman province of Macedonia, was located on the famous Via Egnatia, the main highway connecting Rome with the East.

Paul began his ministry in Thessalonica in the synagogue but eventually turned to Gentiles outside of the synagogue. He wrote 1 Thessalonians from Corinth in late AD 50.

Paul wrote the letter because of his deep concern that the devil would use persecution to destabilize the Thessalonians' young faith. He has six purposes in writing. First, Paul wants to inform the Thessalonians of his great gratitude to God for their spiritual growth (1 Thessalonians 1:2-10). Second, he addresses charges made against him and his missionary team (1 Thessalonians 2:1–3:13), which lie at the center of the letter. One can imagine how Paul's opponents might accuse him of abandoning his followers. Third, Paul writes to encourage these believers in the face of persecution (1 Thessalonians 2:14-16). Fourth, Paul writes to instruct them on several areas of Christian behavior, including sexual purity, loving one another, and the importance of a good work ethic (1 Thessalonians 4:1-12). Fifth, Paul writes

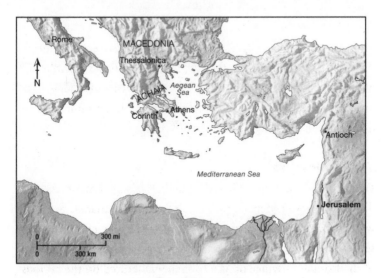

Location of Thessalonica

to provide needed teaching concerning Christ's second coming (1 Thessalonians 4:13–5:11). Sixth, Paul writes to provide instruction on matters related to relationships within the church (1 Thessalonians 5:12-28).

Notice how every chapter in this book ends with a reference to the Second Coming. Though Paul certainly did not include the verse and chapter divisions, this emphasis does highlight the importance of doctrine. Underline every time the phrase "the Good News" or the name of God is used in the book. Without question, 1 Thessalonians centers on the gospel and focuses on God.

Outline

1. Salutation (1 Thessalonians 1:1)

2. Paul's Thanksgiving for the Thessalonians
    (1 Thessalonians 1:2-10)

3. Paul's Defense of His Relationship with the Thessalonians
    (1 Thessalonians 2:1–3:13)

4. Instructions to the Thessalonians (1 Thessalonians
    4:1–5:22)

5. Conclusion (1 Thessalonians 5:23-28)

Digging Into 1 Thessalonians

Salutation (1 Thessalonians 1:1)
Paul includes Silas and Timothy in the salutation because of their role in planting the church.

Paul's Thanksgiving for the Thessalonians
(1 Thessalonians 1:2-10)

Paul gives thanks to God for the good work the Lord is doing in the Thessalonians (1 Thessalonians 1:2-3). As Paul reflects on their spiritual growth, he highlights their faith, hope, and love. He knows God has chosen them because of the way the Good News came to them (1 Thessalonians 1:4-5), the way they received the Good News (1 Thessalonians 1:6-7), and how the Good News "rang out" from them (1 Thessalonians 1:8-10).

Paul's Defense of His Relationship with the Thessalonians
(1 Thessalonians 2:1-3:13)

Paul now takes up one of his main reasons for writing—a lengthy defense of his mission team. Paul's enemies likely attempted to destroy the faith of the Thessalonians by portraying the missionaries as religious charlatans. Paul appeals to the Thessalonians' memories to defend his truthfulness and sincerity (1 Thessalonians 2:1-2, 5, 9-11).

In 1 Thessalonians 2:1-12, Paul recounts the way he conducted himself among the people. He had refused to allow opposition to discourage him (1 Thessalonians 2:1-2). In Philippi, he and his companions had suffered much mistreatment, but rather than keeping quiet in Thessalonica, they kept preaching the gospel, despite opposition. Unlike charlatans, Paul refused to employ unworthy methods or motives, or receive financial compensation from the Thessalonians. On the contrary, Paul and his companions had been tested and approved by God (1 Thessalonians 2:3-6) and worked hard to support themselves (1 Thessalonians 2:7-9). Paul and his associates conducted themselves blamelessly (1 Thessalonians 2:10-12).

In 1 Thessalonians 2:13-16, Paul reminds the Thessalonians

how they received the gospel as the Word of God, even despite persecutions. He says their persecutors greatly displease the Lord.

Paul also wants to put to rest a rumor that he and his friends had no intention of returning to Thessalonica. In fact, their failure to return to Thessalonica had nothing to do with lack of desire (1 Thessalonians 2:17-20). He had not left them voluntarily; he had been torn away from them. In addition, Satan worked to keep him from returning. No one should question Paul's affection for them.

Paul's strong desire to know the welfare of his young converts made him willing to send Timothy, which left Paul alone in Athens (1 Thessalonians 3:1-5). Paul sent Timothy to Thessalonica for three reasons: to stabilize their faith; to encourage them in their faith; and to remind them that all believers will suffer for Christ. Paul could hardly contain himself with the good news Timothy brought back. (By this time, Paul had reached Corinth; see 1 Thessalonians 3:6-10.) Timothy returned with three pieces of good news: the Thessalonians are growing spiritually; they have fond memories of the missionaries; and they long to see their friends again. Paul prays for three specific things for his young converts (1 Thessalonians 3:11-13). First, he prays God would reunite him with them. Second, he prays God will cause their love to abound. (Suffering can tend to make one hard and unkind.) Third, he prays God would grow them in holiness.

Instructions to the Thessalonians (1 Thessalonians 4:1-5:22)

Paul now addresses specific issues in the lives of the Thessalonians. He establishes the supreme principle of Christian living: to please the Lord in all things (1 Thessalonians 4:1-2). Paul identifies three standards by which the Thessalonians can live in a manner pleasing to God:

1. *Maintain sexual purity* (1 Thessalonians 4:3-8). Paul gives four reasons that reveal the importance of this command: God desires their sanctification (1 Thessalonians 4:3); God will punish "all such sins" (1 Thessalonians 4:6); God has called his people to holiness (1 Thessalonians 4:7); and this standard comes from God. To reject the standard is to reject God (1 Thessalonians 4:8).

2. *Love one another* (1 Thessalonians 4:9-10). The Thessalonians have been taught this important truth from the beginning of their Christian life.

3. *Live a quiet, hardworking life—and don't be a busybody* (1 Thessalonians 4:11-12). In this way, "people who are not believers will respect the way you live," which in turn promotes evangelism.

In this section, Paul also deals with two additional matters: the fate of the Christian dead (1 Thessalonians 4:13-18) and the Day of the Lord (1 Thessalonians 5:1-11). As very young believers, the Thessalonians must have wondered what becomes of believers who die before the Second Coming. Not wanting them to remain ignorant about the subject or to grieve like those who have no hope, Paul refers to the Christian dead as having "fallen asleep." Paul does not have in mind a type of soul sleep; rather, as waking up follows sleep, so resurrection follows death. In the next verses, Paul sets forth the knowledge they lack and the reason they should have hope. He affirms that neither Christians still living nor Christians already dead will be left behind or excluded at the Second Coming. Paul sets forth in summary fashion God's eschatological program. The Lord will return at the end of this age in majesty and glory. A shout, the voice of the archangel, and the trumpet of God will accompany Jesus' return. The dead in Christ will rise to meet Jesus first, then those still alive will be caught up together with them to meet the Lord in the air. From then on, the resurrected and the living will be with the Lord forever. Paul did not write to answer academic questions concerning the Second Coming, but rather to encourage his readers.

Next, Paul turns his attention to the Day of the Lord (1 Thessalonians 5:1-11). Some must have thought that the best way to prepare for the Day of the Lord was to know the date, but nobody knows the day or hour. Paul uses two metaphors to describe how the day will come: like a thief in the night (cf. Matthew 24:42; 2 Peter 3:10) and like labor pains upon a pregnant woman. The metaphors teach us that Christ's coming will be both sudden and unavoidable.

If the Day of the Lord will arrive suddenly and unavoidably, then how can the Thessalonians prepare for its arrival? They must prepare by remaining spiritually watchful and alert (1 Thessalonians 5:4-8). They do not need to fear the coming Day of the Lord, because unlike unbelievers, they will not be taken by complete surprise. The unregenerate are like those living in darkness, asleep and drunk. The believer will remain in the light and in the day, spiritually awake. One's lifestyle reflects whether they belong to the day or night. Faith, hope, and love provide the appropriate spiritual armor for the Christian warrior (1 Thessalonians 5:8-10).

Waiting for the return of Christ does not mean idleness, but instead gives an opportunity to serve God's people. Believers are to serve one another. Christians are to love and respect their leaders, while the leaders are to serve, lead, and instruct their flock (1 Thessalonians 5:12-13). Members of the congregation must be mutually accountable to one another (1 Thessalonians 5:14-15); congregational care is not the responsibility only of the leadership.

As a family, believers need to seek one another's spiritual good (1 Thessalonians 5:14-15). Christians must learn to discern how to handle different people and what approach to take with each one: admonish the unruly (undisciplined); encourage the faint-hearted; help the weak; be patient (long-suffering) with everyone. Paul succinctly states the believer's responsibilities toward God. It is God's will that they rejoice always, pray consistently, and give thanks habitually (1 Thessalonians 5:16-18). In 1 Thessalonians 5:19-22, Paul rattles off five commands associated with congregational worship: "Do not stifle the Holy Spirit. Do not scoff at prophecies, but test everything that is said. Hold on to what is good. Stay away from every kind of evil."

Conclusion (1 Thessalonians 5:23-28)

Paul concludes his letter by praying that the Thessalonians might be wholly sanctified. The God who graciously called them to himself will do this wonderful work in them. Paul requests their prayers for him (1 Thessalonians 5:25), having already mentioned three times his prayers for them (1 Thessalonians 1:2; 3:2-13; 5:23). We see Paul's humility, as he requests that his young converts pray on his behalf. The request also demonstrates great confidence in God, that he hears the prayers of all his children, regardless of their spiritual maturity. They are to greet each other warmly. Paul wants the letter read publicly so the entire congregation can benefit from his instruction; Paul sees his letter as a means of discipleship. Finally, he wishes them the grace of Christ. He begins the letter with a prayer for grace and ends the letter in the same way.

Living Out the Message of 1 Thessalonians

This short letter to very young believers in Christ includes important themes that affect the entire Christian life. First, it reminds us that following Jesus does not exempt anyone from persecution and hardship. Paul gives thanks to God for the Thessalonians' resilience. Second, Paul provides important teaching on Christian leadership. Christian leaders must be resilient, God-centered, gospel-focused, and people-oriented rather than project-driven. Leaders are not built in a day, but bit by bit, over time. Third, all believers should understand the Second Coming, even those young in the faith.

14

2 Thessalonians

Be Steadfast

THOSE WHO DELIVERED the letter of 1 Thessalonians to the church reported back to Paul that several of the problems he addressed in his first letter had grown worse. Persecution had intensified, and false teaching concerning Christ's second coming had spread.

The Big Picture

Paul, still in Corinth, could not return in person to Thessalonica to help the young believers. The best he could do was send them another letter addressing key issues.

Paul had three purposes in writing. First, he wanted to encourage his spiritual children to remain resilient in the face of persecution, because when Jesus returns, those who persecuted the church will be judged (2 Thessalonians 1). Second, an error had begun to circulate claiming that the Day of the Lord had already come. Paul confronts this false teaching head-on (2 Thessalonians 2). Third, a group within the church refused to work (2 Thessalonians 3). Paul encouraged the church to deal with these people sternly. As with 1 Thessalonians, Paul wrote the letter from Corinth, penning this one in about AD 52.

Outline

1. Introduction (2 Thessalonians 1:1-4)

2. Doctrinal Exposition: God's Judgment and Christ's Second Coming (2 Thessalonians 1:5–2:12)

3. Practical Exhortations (2 Thessalonians 2:13–3:15)

4. Conclusion (2 Thessalonians 3:16-18)

Digging Into 2 Thessalonians

Introduction (2 Thessalonians 1:1-4)

Like the greeting in 1 Thessalonians, Paul opens his second letter to the church with an expression of thanksgiving for the blessings God has granted them. Paul gives thanks for their spiritual growth, their flourishing faith, and their abundant love (2 Thessalonians 1:3). They have grown despite persecutions and hardships (2 Thessalonians 1:4), which demonstrates they have truly placed their hope in God the Father.

Doctrinal Exposition: God's Judgment and Christ's Second Coming (2 Thessalonians 1:5-2:12)

Paul addresses the continuing suffering in the life of the church, especially in light of two realities: the Thessalonians' spiritual growth and God's future judgment of the persecutors. Paul consistently teaches that through many tribulations, Christians enter the Kingdom of God (Acts 14:22). In suffering, they can feel sure that God is preparing them for glory. God uses the persecutors to develop the Thessalonians' faith, love, and perseverance. The presence of these qualities proves that God considers the Thessalonians worthy of the Kingdom and that he continues to work out his righteous purposes.

One day, God will judge the world for its persecution of the church, and the church will have rest. This judgment will take place when the Lord comes with his mighty angels in flaming fire. Those who do not know God and who refuse to accept the Good News will be punished with eternal destruction and the horror of everlasting alienation from the presence of the Lord. While knowing Christ means eternal life, not knowing him means eternal destruction. The revelation of God's glory to believers and in them will be their reward. As Paul anticipates this event, he prays for his readers to continue in good works for the glory of the Lord (2 Thessalonians 1:11-12).

The church suffered not only at the hand of persecutors, but from false teachers as well (2 Thessalonians 2:1-12). These false teachers seem to have wrongfully taught that Christ's second coming had already occurred. Paul corrects this false teaching by making clear that the Day of the Lord has not yet happened. The Day of the Lord will not take place until a widespread rebellion against God occurs and the "the man of lawlessness" appears. Although Paul does not call this man the Antichrist, surely he has him in mind. The man of lawlessness will exalt himself, challenging God and deceiving unbelievers into following him.

Though the identity of the restrainer who holds back these events is uncertain, God clearly remains in control. The ultimate destiny of the man of lawlessness is destruction (2 Thessalonians 2:8). Those who follow him into rebellion refuse to love the truth and instead choose to believe the lie that the man of lawlessness is divine. In the days when Paul wrote, and still today, the Lord holds in check the power of lawlessness. But a day is coming when the restrainer/restraint will be removed, the man of lawlessness will be revealed, and a great rebellion against God will take place. Nevertheless, a day of retribution will come, as described in chapter 1. The Lord will destroy the Antichrist and those who follow him.

Practical Exhortations (2 Thessalonians 2:13-3:15)

Since Christ will triumph over his enemies, the Thessalonians should stand strong in their faith (2 Thessalonians 2:13-15). The second chapter concludes with a powerful prayer for Paul's spiritual children (2 Thessalonians 2:16-17).

Paul requests the Thessalonians' prayers regarding the spread of God's Word and rescue from wicked people (2 Thessalonians 3:1-5). Paul had immense confidence in the Lord's faithfulness, both for his own protection and the Thessalonians' spiritual growth. Paul assures them that in their affliction, Christ will enable them to persevere.

Paul explains how to handle those in the church who refuse to work (2 Thessalonians 3:6-15). These individuals may have quit working because of an incorrect view that the Day of the Lord had already occurred. Paul frames his argument against idleness first by appealing to the instruction already passed down to them (2 Thessalonians 3:6). He then appeals to them based on the example he had set while still with them. Idleness reveals itself not only in laziness, but also in meddling in other people's business. Paul commands the church to keep a watchful eye on those who continue in idleness and to stay away from them. Believers should instead continue to pursue good works, despite persecution.

Conclusion (2 Thessalonians 3:16-18)

Paul concludes the letter with his autograph as a sign of authenticity. His benediction offers a prayer of blessing on the church for the peace, presence, and grace of the Lord Jesus Christ.

Living Out the Message of 2 Thessalonians

God answers prayer. In 1 Thessalonians 3:10 and 12, Paul had prayed for his young converts to have a maturing faith and a vibrant love, the very qualities for which Paul subsequently expresses gratitude to God in 2 Thessalonians 1:3-4. We often think of faith and love as static, but they can grow and develop, as happened with the Thessalonians despite persecution. Faith and love sometimes grow best in the soil of adversity. Additionally, 2 Thessalonians declares the reality of future judgment. A severe judgment awaits those outside of Christ, and especially those who persecute God's people. Finally, Paul teaches that Jesus will come again in flaming fire, accompanied by angels. Jesus will judge his enemies and be glorified in his people. He will destroy the man of lawlessness (the Antichrist) and judge all those who follow him. The ultimate victory of Jesus, God's Son, assures the final victory of God's people.

15

1 Timothy

Fight the Good Fight!

THE BOOK OF 1 TIMOTHY is known as one of Paul's Pastoral Epistles, along with 2 Timothy and Titus. Though much briefer than many of Paul's other letters, the Pastoral Epistles provide crucial insights on many matters related to the church. The insights in 1 Timothy go far beyond basic issues of church organization and structure to offer helpful counsel on godly living.

The Big Picture

Scholars universally attested to the Pauline authorship of the Pastoral Epistles until the nineteenth century, when some began to suggest that the three letters were pseudonymous. Though pseudonymous writings existed in the ancient world, the early church rejected them as not divinely inspired and consequently did not accept them into the canon of Scripture. The major arguments against Pauline authorship have to do with language (style and vocabulary) and the historical setting of the documents. Though the style of 1 Timothy may differ from Paul's other letters, we lack a large enough sample size to say Paul could not have written it. As for the historical setting, the book of Acts ends with Paul under house arrest in Rome. If he wrote the letter after his release, then we cannot find the setting in Acts. We should accept Pauline authorship because the author claims to be Paul and the early church accepted Pauline authorship. Nothing in the letter excludes Paul as author, and much of the content agrees with the teaching in his other writings.

Paul wrote 1 Timothy after his release from his first Roman imprisonment in AD 62. He likely wrote to Timothy from Macedonia in AD 63, when Timothy lived in Ephesus. Paul has several purposes in writing. First, Paul instructs Timothy to remain in Ephesus and stand firm against false teachers (1 Timothy 1:3-4). Second, the apostle instructs both Timothy and the church on how to conduct themselves in God's household (1 Timothy 3:14-16).

Keep an eye out for five "trustworthy sayings" in the Pastoral Epistles (1 Timothy 1:15; 3:1; 4:9; 2 Timothy 2:11; Titus 3:8). The phrase "trustworthy saying" is found nowhere else in the New Testament. First Timothy features the longest list of qualifications for elders (1 Timothy 3:1-7) and the only list of qualifications for deacons (1 Timothy 3:8-13) in the New Testament. Throughout the letter, note repeated warnings against false teaching and the importance of sound doctrine.

Outline

First Timothy is a personal letter and therefore lacks the formal structure of some of Paul's other letters. Note this lack of strict structure in the following outline.

1. Greeting (1 Timothy 1:1-2)

2. Encouragement and Exhortation (1 Timothy 1:3-20)

3. Instructions for Worship and Leadership in the Church
   (1 Timothy 2:1–3:16)

4. Instructions for Ministry (1 Timothy 4:1-16)

5. Treating Others Well in the Church (1 Timothy 5:1–6:2)

6. Dealing with False Teaching (1 Timothy 6:3-21)

Digging Into 1 Timothy

Greeting (1 Timothy 1:1-2)
Paul's greeting to Timothy follows his standard pattern of author, recipient, and a blessing of grace, mercy, and peace.

Encouragement and Exhortation (1 Timothy 1:3-20)
As Paul launches into his message to Timothy, he writes as one who cares deeply about Timothy and about the believers whom Timothy shepherds. In verses 3-4, Paul sets forth Timothy's primary responsibility:

> When I left for Macedonia, I urged you to stay there
> in Ephesus and stop those whose teaching is contrary
> to the truth. Don't let them waste their time in endless
> discussion of myths and spiritual pedigrees. These things
> only lead to meaningless speculations, which don't help
> people live a life of faith in God.

Paul describes the false teachers as misusing the law of Moses and distorting its intended purpose (1 Timothy 1:6-11). Paul next recounts God's mercy demonstrated in saving him (1 Timothy 1:12-17). The gospel transformed Paul from a sinner to a saint. His salvation reminds us that if God can save someone like Paul, he can save the most hardened of individuals.

The final section in the opening chapter features an exhortation for Timothy to fight well in the Lord's battle against heretical teachers (1 Timothy 1:18-20). If Timothy is to fight well, he must keep his faith focused on Jesus and maintain a good conscience. Hymenaeus and Alexander failed to do this and so shipwrecked their faith. Paul has "handed them over to Satan," hoping they might turn to Christ and stop blaspheming (1 Timothy 1:19-20).

Instructions for Worship and Leadership in the Church (1 Timothy 2:1-3:16)

In chapter 2, Paul turns to practical issues in the church. Prayer must play a major role (1 Timothy 2:1-7). Believers should pray for "all people," especially those in places of governmental authority, so God can work in these people to allow the church to freely spread the gospel without governmental interference and persecution. In public worship gatherings, men should lead out in corporate prayer (1 Timothy 2:8), although the apostle makes it clear in 1 Corinthians 11:5 that women also can pray aloud in public gatherings.

Paul encourages women to dress modestly and to learn quietly within the congregational context (1 Timothy 2:9-15), God's pattern since the creation of Adam and Eve. No one should misconstrue Paul's teaching to suggest that women are inferior to men in any way. Still, male leadership in the church and home is God's plan, providing both structure and order. The verse "But women will be saved through childbearing" (1 Timothy 2:15) is the most difficult statement in this passage. Though many have offered various explanations, the most probable interpretation refers back to God's promise in Genesis 3:15 that through Eve would come One into the world who would crush the serpent's head. The Savior, born from a woman, is the Savior of women.

Paul next turns his attention to elders and deacons (1 Timothy 3:1-13), thus providing Timothy with guidance in selecting church leaders. Those called must be spiritually mature, with lives marked by both attitudes and actions that honor Jesus. Elders must know the Scriptures well enough to teach them; they should have godly homes; they should be mature in the faith and have a reputation for integrity inside and outside the church (1 Timothy 3:1-7). Deacons, likewise, should be selected according to their godly character (1 Timothy 3:8-10, 12-13), while their wives (or deaconesses) are called to equally high standards of integrity and spiritual maturity (1 Timothy 3:11). In 1 Timothy 3:14-15, Paul indicates that he hopes to visit Timothy soon, but if he cannot, he wants his protégé to know how one should conduct oneself in God's household, which is the church of God, "the pillar and foundation of the truth."

Instructions for Ministry (1 Timothy 4:1-16)

In chapter 4, Paul warns Timothy of the certainty of apostasy. Paul does not want Timothy to feel surprised about those who "turn away" from the faith and embrace heretical teaching (1 Timothy 4:1-5). False teaching originates with demons. Paul prescribes sound doctrine and holiness as essential if one is to resist false teachers (1 Timothy 4:6-12). While Timothy had many gifts, godliness must always accompany giftedness, for giftedness is not the same as maturity. Some very gifted people lack godly character and so have brought disrepute to the church. Timothy must pay close attention to both his doctrine and his life (1 Timothy 4:13-15). Verse 16 emphasizes that the salvation of others is at stake in Timothy's godly living and orthodox teaching. When shepherds give attention to their own spiritual lives, they can minister more effectively to others.

Treating Others Well in the Church (1 Timothy 5:1–6:2)

Paul addresses various age groups within the church from the perspective of a family (1 Timothy 5:1-4). Timothy should relate to older men with love, respect, and gentleness; younger men as brothers; older women as mothers; and younger women with all purity. In verses 5-16, Paul instructs Timothy how to determine if the church should financially support widows. This lengthy section reminds us that the church must have great concern for widows. In the ancient world, women whose spouses died were often left destitute.

Timothy returns to the issue of elders, especially those who preach and teach the Word. The church should compensate them well for their faithful ministry (1 Timothy 5:17-18). In addition, no one should irresponsibly accuse elders of wrongdoing; at least two witnesses must agree on any accusation against an elder (1 Timothy 5:19-20). Elders examined for wrongdoing should not be treated with favoritism because of their position (1 Timothy 5:21), which explains why elders must be spiritually mature with a track record of godly living (1 Timothy 5:24-25). In 1 Timothy 6:1-2, Paul addresses the relationship between slaves and masters. Every believer has certain responsibilities to God that should inform how they interact with one another.

Dealing with False Teaching (1 Timothy 6:3-21)

Paul returns once again to the subject of false teachers, whose doctrine contradicts Scripture. False teaching inevitably results in ungodly living and contentious behavior. Many false teachers crave financial gain (1 Timothy 6:3-5). Personal godliness must accompany doctrinal orthodoxy. Believers must not lust for material wealth (1 Timothy 6:6-10). Timothy must flee worldliness and pursue the things of God (1 Timothy 6:11-16). The wealthy should use their God-given resources for God's glory (1 Timothy 6:17-19).

Paul concludes his letter with a few well-worded admonitions. Timothy must guard the gospel and avoid false teaching and unnecessary argumentation. Some who have failed to follow this advice have fallen away.

Living Out the Message of 1 Timothy

Discipleship has a vitally important role to play in the church. Paul discipled Timothy. To some degree, Timothy became the man he was because of Paul's investment in his life. The church cannot advance the Kingdom without good discipleship. Timothy could make a big impact for the Kingdom because Paul invested in his life.

Next, 1 Timothy teaches us the importance of sound doctrine. Bad theology leads to bad living. Sound doctrine is built on the truths of Scripture. The church needs well-grounded Christians who know their Bibles, who read books of substance, and who live out the teachings of Scripture. Sloppy thinking leads to sloppy living.

Finally, the church needs godly leadership. Paul spends considerable time instructing Timothy on this subject. Leaders should have both a mature understanding of the truth and godly lifestyles. We should not choose leaders based on an attractive personality or the length of their church membership. Paul plainly states the requirements for elders and deacons. Many problems in our churches stem from choosing gifted men to lead who lack personal holiness of character.

16

2 Timothy

Final Words

SECOND TIMOTHY, ANOTHER of Paul's Pastoral Epistles, is the final letter he wrote before his execution. Paul is lonely and cold. He yearns to see his son in the faith before his death. This time, Paul is not imprisoned in rented quarters, as in his first Roman imprisonment, but in a cold and dark dungeon. The great missionary theologian of the early church is likely just days from execution.

The Big Picture

Paul's letter to his close associate Timothy reminds us that the world seldom recognizes true greatness. Paul, the greatest missionary theologian in the history of the church, spends his final days in a Roman prison. The world has treated God's people the same way throughout the ages. Herod's soldier decapitated John the Baptist. Roman soldiers crucified Jesus. Peter also eventually died by crucifixion.

Paul wrote this letter during his second Roman imprisonment in approximately AD 65 or 66.[11] Timothy was likely still in Ephesus. The winter chill in the Roman prison caused Paul to desire his cloak. Paul understood his time had grown short, and he longed for the companionship of Timothy (and John Mark).

Paul had at least two purposes in writing. First, he felt lonely, and he wanted to see Timothy before his execution (2 Timothy 1:15; 4:9-12). Second, as always, Paul was concerned about the gospel. He wanted Timothy to guard the gospel (2 Timothy 1:14), to persevere in the gospel (2 Timothy 3:14), to continue preaching the Word (2 Timothy 4:2), and, if necessary, to suffer for the gospel (2 Timothy 1:8; 2:3).

As you read 2 Timothy, look for statements that reflect Paul's situation. For example, he sits in a cold dungeon, chained like a common prisoner and deserted by so-called friends. Also, look for what Paul says about the importance of a theological heritage. God can use parents and grandparents to bring a son and grandson to faith in Christ. But most importantly, look for what Paul says about the gospel and sound doctrine.

Outline

1. Salutation and Thanksgiving (2 Timothy 1:1-5)

2. Paul's Initial Ministerial Charges to Timothy (2 Timothy 1:6–2:13)

3. Contrast in the Church (2 Timothy 2:14-26)

4. Paul's Charge to Withstand the Coming Apostasy (2 Timothy 3:1-17)

5. Paul's Final Charges (2 Timothy 4:1-8)

6. Concluding Thoughts and Final Farewells (2 Timothy 4:9-22)

Digging Into 2 Timothy

Salutation and Thanksgiving (2 Timothy 1:1-5)

Paul's opening lines do not sound like a man facing execution. He sees himself as a chosen apostle of Jesus Christ (2 Timothy 1:1-2). Despite his situation, he has a calling to tell others about Jesus. He wants Timothy to experience the grace, mercy, and peace of God.

Paul's Initial Ministerial Charges to Timothy (2 Timothy 1:6-2:13)

Paul launches into his first round of directives to Timothy, his understudy. He recalls the significant influence Timothy's mother and grandmother have had in his life (2 Timothy 1:5-6). Considering that influence, Timothy must use his spiritual gift in God's service. The remainder of the first chapter exhorts Timothy not to be ashamed of the gospel (2 Timothy 1:8-18) but rather to follow Paul's example (2 Timothy 1:8-14). Despite the apostle's imprisonment for preaching the gospel, and although many had abandoned him, God's grace must continue to be proclaimed. Onesiphorus provides a shining example of one not ashamed of Paul or of the gospel (2 Timothy 1:15-18).

Paul calls Timothy to be strong in service to King Jesus (2 Timothy 2:1-7). After stating the charge to make disciples (2 Timothy 2:1-2), Paul illustrates Christian discipleship with the images of a soldier, an athlete, and a farmer. Jesus gives us the ultimate example of suffering before glory (2 Timothy 2:8-13). Verses 11-13 present one of Paul's trustworthy sayings.

Contrast in the Church (2 Timothy 2:14-26)

Paul draws three contrasts, the first of which is between true and false teachers (2 Timothy 2:14-19). Faithful workers in God's Kingdom are committed to the truths of God's Word and to the pursuit of holiness. Second, Paul contrasts honorable and dishonorable vessels (2 Timothy 2:20-22). Holiness distinguishes one from the other. Third, Paul distinguishes between the kind and the quarrelsome (2 Timothy 2:23-26). An argumentative and contentious disposition may indicate a false teacher.

Paul's Charge to Withstand the Coming Apostasy (2 Timothy 3:1-17)

Paul's description of the last days remains as true today as in the first century. People will love anything and everything other than God (2 Timothy 3:1-5). False teachers will take advantage of the unsuspecting. Judgment, however, will come to them (2 Timothy 3:6-9). Paul bases his charge to Timothy on what Timothy already knows of Paul's teaching and how the apostle has suffered for the gospel. Everyone who desires to live a godly life will suffer in this ungodly world. Those who persecute God's people will themselves suffer God's judgment (2 Timothy 3:10-13). Timothy, however, must remain faithful to what he has been taught. God has graciously provided his inspired Word to prepare and equip God's people to serve him (2 Timothy 3:14-17).

Paul's Final Charges (2 Timothy 4:1-8)

In 2 Timothy 4:1-8, we have Paul's final ministerial charges to Timothy. Timothy is to preach the Word (2 Timothy 4:1-5), a charge that comes with the greatest solemnity (2 Timothy 4:1). Timothy must always be prepared to preach the Word, working hard to apply its truths to the lives of his hearers (2 Timothy

4:2). A day will come when people will reject the truth of God's Word (2 Timothy 4:3-4). Until then, Timothy must proclaim the Word, even if it results in suffering (2 Timothy 4:5). Verses 6-8 are some of the most famous words Paul ever wrote. Paul's faithfulness should encourage Timothy to remain faithful. Paul has faithfully run his race and will soon receive his reward—something true not only of Paul, but of all who faithfully run their God-appointed race.

Concluding Thoughts and Final Farewells (2 Timothy 4:9-22)

Paul concludes his final letter by encouraging Timothy to come quickly. Paul feels lonely and wants Timothy to bring John Mark along with him. Tychicus will replace Timothy in Ephesus. Paul also instructs Timothy to bring Paul's cloak, books, and parchments. Timothy must beware of Alexander the coppersmith (2 Timothy 4:14-15), likely the same "Alexander" mentioned in 1 Timothy 1:20. Paul informs Timothy of his present legal situation (2 Timothy 4:16-18). Then he bids final greetings and farewell. We do not know if Timothy arrived in Rome before Paul's execution. We do know Paul did not die alone; Jesus remained with him to the very end.

Living Out the Message of 2 Timothy

Second Timothy reminds us that living for Jesus can be dangerous. The Romans executed Paul for preaching the gospel. For Paul, the gospel mattered more than his life. Timothy must also be willing to suffer for the gospel. We often feel more concerned about living comfortably than being faithful witnesses of the gospel. Casual Christianity, which is not Christianity at all, feels no compulsion to provide a gospel witness.

Paul's final letter also reminds us of the importance of parental discipleship, which begins in the home. Every parent whose spouse does not know Jesus should feel encouraged by the influence Timothy's mother and grandmother had on him. Timothy lacked the influence of a dad who knew Christ, yet he came to faith in Jesus and joined Paul's mission team. The faithful ministry of his mother and grandmother led to his conversion.

Finally, we recall the importance of a Word-centered ministry. Paul offered his instruction to Timothy to preach the Word with great solemnity: "I solemnly urge you in the presence of God and Christ Jesus, who will someday judge the living and the dead when he comes to set up his Kingdom: Preach the word of God. Be prepared, whether the time is favorable or not. Patiently correct, rebuke, and encourage your people with good teaching" (2 Timothy 4:1-2). In modern life, preaching has fallen on hard times. Many in the pews clamor for shorter sermons, filled with funny stories and anecdotes, and many in the pulpit are far too eager to oblige. In a day when many see the proclamation of truth as fanatical indoctrination, the church must have preachers who believe the Bible is the Word of God, fully sufficient for faith and practice. Preaching and discipleship must be Word-centered if they are to transform anyone.

17

Titus

Engage in Good Works

THE BOOK OF TITUS is yet another of Paul's Prison Epistles. Titus, one of the lesser-known figures in the New Testament, was a trusted companion of the apostle Paul. When the Jerusalem leadership sought to determine the status of Gentiles, Paul took Titus into that tense setting as a test case (Galatians 2:1-3). Paul entrusted Titus with a sorrowful letter to the Corinthians and then tasked him with making sure the Corinthians had prepared to give a promised generous offering to the Jerusalem saints (2 Corinthians 7:5-14; 8:6). When someone needed to oversee the difficult work on Crete, Paul once again called on Titus. Paul had the utmost confidence in this faithful man.

The Big Picture

Titus had come to faith through Paul's ministry (Titus 1:4). Paul commissioned Titus to remain on Crete as his representative and complete some needed work there (Titus 1:5; 2:15; 3:12-13). Titus then should meet Paul at Nicopolis (on the west coast of Greece) once a replacement arrived for him on Crete (Titus 3:12). Later, Titus went on a mission to Dalmatia, the last time we hear of him in the New Testament (2 Timothy 4:10). Titus appears to have been a capable and resourceful leader.

Crete, the fourth largest island in the Mediterranean Sea, lies directly south of the Aegean Sea. Paul spent time there on his journey to Rome (Acts 27:7-13). In New Testament times, Crete had sunk to a deplorably low moral level. Paul left Titus on Crete to help organize the churches. Paul sent his letter to Titus by Zenas and Apollos, then on a journey that took them through Crete (Titus 3:13). The letter instructs Titus how to handle opposition (Titus 1:5, 7-8, 15; 3:9). Paul offers Titus instruction about faith and conduct. In addition, Paul warns about false teachers and informs Titus about his plans for the future. Few question Pauline authorship of Titus. We do not know for certain from what location Paul wrote the letter, but he may have written it from Corinth before leaving for Nicopolis. He likely wrote the letter between AD 63 and 65.

Paul had at least four purposes in writing to Titus: first, to instruct Titus on establishing leadership in the Cretan churches; second, to confront false teachers endangering the church; third, to advise Titus to join Paul before winter, as soon as Artemis or Tychicus visited; and fourth, to encourage the church on Crete to perform good works.

Look for several characteristics as you read the letter. First, Paul emphasizes the importance of good works (Titus 1:16; 2:14; 3:1, 8, 14). Second, he uses the word *Savior* six times, three times to refer to God the Father (Titus 1:3; 2:10; 3:4) and three times to Jesus (Titus 1:4; 2:13; 3:6). Third, a deep evangelistic passion lies behind Paul's ethical instructions (Titus 2:8, 10). Fourth, sound doctrine demands right conduct, regardless of the age of the believer (Titus 2:2-10). Finally, Paul gives two classic summaries of Christian doctrine (Titus 2:11-14; 3:4-7).

Outline

1. Salutation (Titus 1:1-4)

2. Qualifications for Elders (Titus 1:5-9)

3. Warnings concerning False Teachers (Titus 1:10-16)

4. Instructions for Various Age Groups (Titus 2:1-10)

5. Instructions concerning Christian Living (Titus 2:11–3:11)

6. Greetings and Final Instructions (Titus 3:12-15)

Digging Into Titus

Salutation (Titus 1:1-4)

Paul gives quite a robust greeting to Titus (Titus 1:1-4). After all his years of ministry, Paul remains clear about his calling: to preach the gospel to the lost and disciple the saints. Believers cannot live in a godly way without knowing the truth. Paul refers to God as Savior, unique to the Pastoral Epistles. In verse 4, he refers to Jesus as Savior.

Qualifications for Elders (Titus 1:5-9)

Paul offers guidance to Titus on the selection of elders. Paul left Titus on Crete, in part, to appoint elders to the churches. A man appointed to the position of elder must be spiritually mature and display a godly life. The book of Titus first sets forth the responsibility of elders and then the qualifications for elders (Titus 1:6-9). Elders must be chosen based upon their spiritual maturity and not because of their congregational popularity.

Warnings concerning False Teachers (Titus 1:10-16)

One reason the church needs qualified leadership is because of the danger of false teachers. The ungodly character of false teachers diametrically opposes the godliness of the elders Titus is to appoint. In verses 10-13, Paul sets forth the character and conduct of false teachers, and in verses 14-16, their false teaching. The false teachers advocate a false spirituality through asceticism (Titus 1:11-16).

Instructions for Various Age Groups (Titus 2:1-10)

After establishing Titus's responsibility (Titus 2:1), Paul sets forth instructions for various age groups of men and women (Titus 2:2-8). The church, as a family, must demonstrate "family values" in its interactions with one another. The apostle Paul wanted all believers to see the church as a family. He goes on to give instructions for the workplace setting (Titus 2:9-10).

Instructions concerning Christian Living (Titus 2:11-3:11)

In Titus 2:11–3:11, Paul offers instructions on Christian living. Godly living must always be grounded in solid theology (Titus 2:11-15). God's grace appeared with the incarnation of Jesus (Titus 2:11). As a result, believers must reject godlessness as they await Christ's second coming (Titus 2:12-13). God's grace produces within God's people a longing for Christ's return. Paul refers to Jesus as both God and Savior. Jesus died to cleanse his people from sin, to free them from slavery to sin, and to perform good deeds (Titus 2:14).

Paul instructs Christians about their relationship to the

government and to all people (Titus 3:1-2). Godly living has two main motivations. First, we must recall our past spiritual condition (Titus 3:3). Second, we must understand our present salvation (Titus 3:4-7). Paul provides a beautiful summary of the gospel. The incarnation of Jesus manifested the gospel (Titus 3:4). God's mercy provides the basis of salvation (Titus 3:5) while the cleansing and regenerating work of the Holy Spirit provides the means of salvation (Titus 3:5-6). Paul delineates the results of salvation in 3:7-8. In practical living, salvation manifests itself to others through good works. As the letter concludes, Paul exhorts his readers to shun those who continually engage in foolish controversies and behave in a divisive manner.

Greetings and Final Instructions (Titus 3:12-15)
Paul offers some concluding instructions to his trusted friend. Paul also gives one more admonition to engage in good works.

Living Out the Message of Titus
As mentioned, Titus uses the word *Savior* six times, three times of God the Father and three times of Jesus. What does this mean? Paul refers to both God the Father and Jesus Christ the Son as Savior, highlighting the equality and unity of the Father and Son. We do not have two separate Saviors; we should not think of God as one of our Saviors and of Jesus as our other Savior. The singular expression *our Savior* applies equally to both, yet does not result in more than one Savior. Also, it underscores the unity of the Father and Son in the work of redemption. Jesus did not carry out the work of redemption against the Father's will. The Father and the Son acted in a shared love to bring about our salvation. Our understanding of God the Father as Savior and Christ the Son as Savior should deepen our worship.

Next, good works do not come naturally to most of us. Paul exhorted Titus on several occasions to encourage good works among his people. We often think of good works as works we perform at church, but good works include anything we do for the glory of God. A good work is mowing the lawn for a sick neighbor, for God's glory. A good work is visiting a nursing home to serve an aging parent or friend, for God's glory.

Finally, we need more believers like Titus. Titus lived in Paul's shadow, but he never seemed to mind. His more famous friend could always count on him. People in ministry often long to be on the main stage, but the church needs more people like Titus, who embrace God's calling even in a supporting role.

18

Philemon

A Call to Forgiveness

PHILEMON, PAUL'S SHORTEST LETTER in the New Testament, is only twenty-five verses long. But what a potent and relevant message it conveys! The theme of forgiveness sounds forth between the lines of this brief letter.

The Big Picture

Several names found in both Philemon and Colossians appear to closely link these two books: Timothy, Aristarchus, Mark, Demas, Luke, Archippus, and Onesimus. Philemon, the recipient of the letter, must have lived in Colossae. The book of Philemon is another of Paul's Prison Epistles. Paul wrote to Philemon while imprisoned in Rome in AD 61 and dispatched it, along with Colossians, to be delivered by Tychicus (Colossians 4:7).

Onesimus appears to have been a runaway slave who made his way to Rome, where he providentially encountered Paul and was saved. Paul encouraged him to return home and entrusted Tychicus with a letter to Philemon, asking him to receive Onesimus as if he were Paul.

Outline

1. Paul's Greeting (Philemon 1:1-3)

2. Paul's Commendation of Philemon (Philemon 1:4-7)

3. Paul's Request of Philemon for Onesimus (Philemon 1:8-17)

4. Paul's Promise to Philemon (Philemon 1:18-22)

5. Paul's Final Greetings (Philemon 1:23-25)

Digging Into Philemon

Paul's Greeting (Philemon 1:1-3)
Paul's rather standard greeting mentions his imprisonment for preaching the Good News, a subtle reminder to Philemon of Paul's willingness to suffer for the gospel. The apostle writes to Philemon, Apphia (likely Philemon's wife), and Archippus (possibly Philemon's and Apphia's son). Paul also wants the letter read to the church that meets in their home. Such a public reading puts pressure on Philemon to do the right thing regarding Onesimus. Paul prays for grace and peace for them.

Paul's Commendation of Philemon (Philemon 1:4-7)
Paul gives thanks to God for Philemon's Christian character. Philemon is known for his faith in Jesus and his love for God's

people, and Paul prays that Philemon will demonstrate his spiritual maturity by a spirit of generosity. Philemon's generosity has refreshed Paul and many others already.

Paul's Request of Philemon for Onesimus (Philemon 1:8-17)

Paul requests that Philemon, his brother in Christ, perform a favor for him. He could command him to do it, considering his apostolic authority and the appropriateness of the request, but he prefers that Philemon obey freely and do nothing under compulsion. Paul reminds him of their deep friendship, the fact that Paul is now an old man and a prisoner for the gospel (the second mention of his imprisonment). He asks Philemon to show kindness toward his spiritual child, Onesimus. Apparently, Paul led Onesimus to faith in Rome. Up to this point, Onesimus had not been very useful to Philemon. Paul makes a play on words here, for the name Onesimus means "beneficial" or "useful." Though before his conversion Onesimus had not been useful to Philemon, now that he is a child of God, his uselessness has been transformed into usefulness. Returning Onesimus to Philemon tears at Paul's heart, demonstrating the apostle's love for this young brother in Christ.

For a third time, Paul reminds Philemon of his imprisonment (Philemon 1:13). Onesimus had helped Paul in Rome, but the apostle does not want him to remain without Philemon's permission. Once again, Paul applies a subtle (or not so subtle) form of pressure. Paul hopes Onesimus will help Paul willingly and not by a sense of undue pressure. Onesimus is no longer merely a slave to Philemon; he is a brother in Christ. Though the two of them had been temporarily separated, they now have an eternal bond in Christ. Paul adds to the gospel pressure he puts on Philemon by asking him to receive Onesimus as he would receive Paul himself.

The entire congregation meeting in Philemon's home must have looked at their host and wondered how he would respond.

Paul's Promise to Philemon (Philemon 1:18-22)

If Philemon has suffered any financial loss because of Onesimus, Paul will repay him. Paul then reminds Philemon of his great debt to the apostle. Again, Paul pushes Philemon to do the right thing. Paul may be Philemon's spiritual father, just as with Onesimus. Either way, Philemon owes Paul a great spiritual debt for Paul's ministry to him and to his family. Paul wants him to do this great favor for God's glory and Paul's encouragement.

Paul has great confidence in his spiritual brother, Philemon, that he will do not only what Paul has requested, but much more. After Paul's release from prison, he hopes to visit Philemon and stay in his home. Then they can renew their friendship and Paul can feel greatly encouraged by his friend's positive response to his requests.

Paul's Final Greetings (Philemon 1:23-25)

Paul mentions several names that tie this letter to Colossians and then concludes with a blessing of grace.

Living Out the Message of Philemon

Think of this short letter as a powerful call to Christian forgiveness. Though Paul does not use the word *forgiveness*, we see the concept throughout. Paul uses godly persuasion to encourage Philemon not to hold Onesimus's sins against him. Paul desires that Philemon treat Onesimus in the same way he would treat the apostle, a direct assault against the sin of partiality. We do not know how Philemon responded, but based on Paul's strong commendation of him in the early sections of the letter, Philemon very likely received Onesimus just as he would have received Paul. The church is a family, and family members should treat one another as brothers and sisters in Christ.

PART III

The General Letters and Revelation

THE FINAL SECTION of the New Testament, the general letters, were not written to specific recipients. Though Paul names the churches and individuals to whom he writes, the general epistles refer to their recipients in more general terms. Therefore, most of these books take the name of the writer. The letters of 2 John and 3 John are exceptions to this pattern, because John addresses these short letters to specific individuals. Hebrews also deviates from this model, because we don't know the identity of the author and he addresses a specific audience (Hebrews 5:11–6:12).

The author of Hebrews wrote to encourage suffering Jewish Christians to resist the temptation to return to Judaism. James is the New Testament version of Proverbs, written to Jewish Christians persecuted by fellow Jews of a higher social standing. First Peter was written to strengthen both Jewish and Gentile believers suffering some local persecution. Second Peter and Jude were written to combat an onslaught of false teaching. The apostle John wrote his three letters to encourage his readers to love one another and hold to the truth. Though some of these letters seem more like postcards than lengthy treatises, they are extremely powerful.

The final book in the New Testament is Revelation (*not* Revelations). Revelation offers a perfect conclusion to the Bible. The book interprets past and present events, as well as offering a stunning description of the final events of human history. If you have never read Revelation, (spoiler alert) God wins! The book presents many interpretive difficulties because it uses a great deal of imagery unfamiliar to contemporary readers. But once we understand those images from a first-century perspective, Revelation becomes much easier to grasp. I advise you not to give up on Revelation, which God included in the Bible to inspire hope in its readers.

19

Hebrews

Jesus Is Greater

Many Christians find Hebrews a difficult book because of its heavy use of the Old Testament. Yet, no book in the New Testament has more to say on the high priesthood of Jesus than Hebrews. Though the book may seem complex, we must strive to understand its message to better grasp Christ's person and work.

The Big Picture

We do not know who wrote Hebrews; its authorship is one of the great mysteries of New Testament studies. Though scholars throughout the centuries have suggested many candidates—Luke, Silas, Apollos, Barnabas, and Paul—the book is anonymous and provides no clear insight into the writer's identity.

Certain facts about the author, however, seem clear. For instance, the author is a second-generation Christian (Hebrews 2:3). His grasp of the Greek language and of the Old Testament suggests he is a Jewish Christian of the diaspora. His Old Testament quotations come from the Septuagint (LXX), the Greek translation of the Hebrew Scriptures (not surprising, considering the author's grasp of the Greek language). Though we cannot identify the author, his readers clearly knew him (Hebrews 13:18-19).

Neither do we clearly know the exact identity of the letter's recipients. The author plainly wrote to a specific audience, and he appears very familiar with the dangers of their present circumstances (cf. Hebrews 10:32-34). The letter's abundance of Old Testament references suggests an audience primarily of Jewish Christians.

Why the author wrote seems clearer. The recipients had put their faith in Christ (Hebrews 3:1; 10:32) but were in danger of drifting away (Hebrews 2:1). Apparently, they were suffering persecution for their faith in Christ (Hebrews 10:32-39). They may have been considering reverting to Judaism, which would explain the constant reminder that Jesus is better. The author wants to warn his readers of the danger of apostasy and the superiority of the person and work of Christ.

A date for the writing of the book sometime between AD 64 and 68 seems likely. Timothy is clearly still alive (Hebrews 13:23). The Temple does not appear to have been destroyed, and the sacrificial system appears to still be in place. The Romans razed the Temple in AD 70, and at that time the sacrificial system came to an end.

As you read Hebrews, spend time looking up the author's numerous Old Testament quotes and allusions. Hebrews provides a window into how first-century Jewish Christians read and interpreted the Hebrew Scriptures. You will find strategically placed warnings to readers encouraging them to persevere in the faith. These passages provide striking reminders that the Christian life is filled with many trials. Only by keeping our eyes on Jesus, the author and finisher of our faith (Hebrews 12:2, KJV), can we fortify our souls against the troubles of this life.

Finally, before digging into Hebrews, notice that it does not begin like a typical first-century letter. Observe the lack of a traditional introduction (similar to 1 John). The book ends, however, in a more letter-like fashion. Hebrews reads more like an extended sermon than an epistle. The author calls it a "brief exhortation" (Hebrews 13:22).

Outline

1. Jesus Is Greater than the Old Testament Prophets (Hebrews 1:1-3)

2. Jesus Is Greater than the Angels (Hebrews 1:4–2:18)

3. Jesus Is Greater than Moses (Hebrews 3:1-19)

4. Jesus Is Greater than Joshua (Hebrews 4:1-13)

5. Jesus Is Greater than Aaron (Hebrews 4:14–10:18)

6. Jesus Is Greater as the New and Living Way (Hebrews 10:19–13:25)

Digging Into Hebrews

Jesus Is Greater than the Old Testament Prophets (Hebrews 1:1-3)

This book could not have begun in a grander fashion. The author begins by establishing that Jesus is greater than the Old Testament prophets. What the writer says about the Son in these verses could never be said of any mere prophet. Though the author acknowledges that God has spoken in the past through the prophets, the revelation through Jesus is far superior to that of the prophets.

Jesus Is Greater than the Angels (Hebrews 1:4–2:18)

The author next turns his attention to Jesus' superiority to the angels. The writer does not disparage the significance of angels, for God created them to serve his people (Hebrews 1:14). But the contrast between the angels and Jesus could not be greater. Jesus is God's Son, while God created angels to worship and serve him (Hebrews 1:5-6). In verses 5-14, the author strings together a series of Old Testament verses to corroborate the Son's superiority to angels.

Because of the Son's superiority to angels, one must pay careful attention to what the Son says. In Hebrews 2:1-4, the author introduces the first of several warning passages scattered throughout the book. Readers must give heed to whatever Christ speaks and to the salvation he offers. To ignore the warnings will result in severe judgment.

The writer next uses Psalm 8:4-6 to transition from his discussion of Jesus' divinity to his humanity (Hebrews 2:5-9). In verses 10-18, the author establishes Christ's work on behalf of human beings. The writer's argument unfolds in three thoughts, all of which emphasize Christ's humanity. First, the Son had to share our humanity to bring us to God (Hebrews 2:10). Second, Christ had to share our humanity to defeat our enemy, the devil (Hebrews 2:14-15). Third, the Son had to share our humanity to become a fully qualified high priest (Hebrews 2:16-18).

Jesus Is Greater than Moses (Hebrews 3:1-19)

Jesus is *vastly* greater than Moses. Though Moses was a servant in God's household, Jesus is God's Son (Hebrews 3:1-6). This comparison leads into the second warning passage (Hebrews 3:7-19), centering around Psalm 95:7-11 and its relevance for readers (Hebrews 3:7-11). The passage gives a sobering reminder of the unfaithfulness of God's people during their wilderness wanderings. The passage also stresses the importance of listening to the voice of God (cf. Hebrews 2:1-4). The author points to Israel's experience in Numbers 14:1-35 to illustrate the dangerous consequences of unbelief and disobedience (Hebrews 3:12-19).

Jesus Is Greater than Joshua (Hebrews 4:1-13)

The author next turns his attention to Moses' successor, Joshua. As great a leader as Joshua was, he failed to lead Israel into God's rest because of their disobedience (Hebrews 4:2-3, 11). Jesus offers genuine rest to his people if they believe the gospel and embrace its promises (Hebrews 4:9-10). We encounter three ideas of "rest" in this passage. The first refers to the rest of the Promised Land, while the second speaks of Sabbath rest. Both are mere shadows of God's ultimate rest, which begins in this life through salvation in Christ but is not fully experienced until eternity.

Jesus Is Greater than Aaron (Hebrews 4:14-10:18)

The length of this section of Hebrews suggests its significance. The author begins with a description of Jesus' work as our high priest, representing his people in God's presence (Hebrews 4:14–5:10). The writer describes the general qualifications for the high priest (Hebrews 5:1-4) and then presents Christ's qualifications (Hebrews 5:5-10).

The next passage establishes the danger of prolonged spiritual immaturity (Hebrews 5:11–6:12). This section falls naturally into four parts.

The first part (Hebrews 5:11-14) warns of the danger of failing to progress in one's spiritual life because of dullness of hearing (cf.

Hebrews 2:1-4; 4:7). Though by this point the recipients of the letter should be mature enough to be teaching others about the Christian faith, the writer says, instead they still need to be taught the basic principles themselves.

The second part (Hebrews 6:1-3) exhorts readers to spiritual maturity. It sets forth the path before them in two exhortations: "let us stop" and "let us go on."

The third part (Hebrews 6:4-8) establishes the terrifying danger of apostasy and describes those who are in jeopardy: "those who were once enlightened . . . and who then turn away from God" (Hebrews 6:4-6).

The remainder of Hebrews 6:6 is notoriously difficult: "It is impossible to bring such people back to repentance; by rejecting the Son of God, they themselves are nailing him to the cross once again and holding him up to public shame." Scholars suggest three major views on this verse. How we interpret this passage will likely govern our understanding of all the warning passages in Hebrews.

The first interpretation suggests that the author refers to genuine Christians who fall away from the faith, a sin considered so egregious they may never come back. This view contradicts the New Testament teaching of the believer's eternal security in Christ (see John 6:37, 39; 10:28-30; Romans 8:31-39). A second interpretation calls the warning hypothetical. Those who hold this position suggest that such apostasy has never actually happened. But unless the writer is speaking of a real possibility, it's not much of a warning. The third interpretation claims that the author is referring to professing Christians whose apostasy proves the spurious nature of their faith. Judas Iscariot is an example of a man who appeared to have genuine faith, but who in the end clearly did not. This third interpretation sees verses 7-8 as a parable that graphically illustrates the meaning of the warning.

The final part of this section (Hebrews 6:9-20) encourages the Hebrews to persevere. The writer reminds them of the Old Testament hero Abraham as an example of trust and endurance (Hebrews 6:13-20).

In Hebrews 7:1-10, the author returns to the nature of Christ's priesthood. Christ's priesthood is after the order of Melchizedek (Genesis 14:17-20). As great as Abraham was in his role as the father of the Jewish people, Melchizedek is greater. Melchizedek's name and hometown suggest that he was both the "king of righteousness" and the "king of peace." The Scriptures record no events associated with the beginning or ending of Melchizedek's life, and the author uses this omission to teach that Melchizedek has an eternal priesthood, like that of Christ (Hebrews 7:1-3). Abraham's payment of tithes to Melchizedek shows that the priest was greater than Abraham (Hebrews 7:4-10).

In Hebrews 7:11-28, the writer proves that Christ's priesthood is superior to the Aaronic priesthood, based on six propositions. First, Christ's priesthood is greater because he is both priest and king, thus having a royal priesthood (Hebrews 7:11-14). Second, Christ's priesthood is greater because of the permanence of his life. Jewish high priests died and had to be replaced, unlike Christ, who lives forever (Hebrews 7:15-17). Third, Christ's priesthood is greater because he gives his people direct access to God. Jewish high priests only represented the people before God (Hebrews 7:18-19). Fourth, Christ's priesthood is greater because it establishes God's oath. As a result of this oath, Jesus provides a better covenant (Hebrews 7:20-22). Fifth, Christ's priesthood is greater because the priesthood is final and unchangeable (Hebrews 7:23-25). Sixth, Christ's priesthood is greater because Christ offers himself as an eternal, infinitely efficacious sacrifice (Hebrews 7:26-28).

In Hebrews 8:1–10:18, the writer focuses attention on the superiority of the work of Christ. He bases his argument for this section on Jeremiah 31:31-34 and demonstrates that Christ is the mediator of a better covenant. We can see the superiority of Christ's work in that his ministry is a heavenly one (Hebrews 8:1-5) that mediates a better covenant (Hebrews 8:6-13). The new covenant has superior blessings: (1) God's law becomes an inner principle enabling God's people to delight in obeying God; (2) God and his people enjoy more intimate fellowship with one another; (3) sinful ignorance of God's will is removed; (4) forgiveness of sins becomes an everlasting reality; and (5) God himself will teach his people.

As high priest, Christ serves in a better sanctuary (Hebrews 9:1-12). The old sanctuary (the Tabernacle) was arranged in a particular way (Hebrews 9:1-5). The sacrifices offered at the Tabernacle were not eternally effectual (Hebrews 9:6-10), which pointed forward to a better sacrifice. Christ serves in a better sanctuary and offers an eternally effectual sacrifice (Hebrews 9:11-12).

In Hebrews 9:13–10:18, the author proves that Christ offers a better sacrifice. First, Christ's sacrifice is better because he, as victim, is superior to the Old Testament animal sacrifices (Hebrews 9:13-14). Second, Christ's sacrifice is superior because the sacrifice establishes a new and better covenant (Hebrews 9:15-22). And third, the sacrifice is eternally efficacious (Hebrews 9:23-28). Finally, Christ provides the only perfect sacrifice for sin (Hebrews 10:1-18). The sacrifices offered by the Jewish high priests on the Day of Atonement could never provide perfect cleansing. The once-for-all death of Jesus takes away the sins of God's people forever. Since those sins are perfectly atoned for, no further need exists for animal sacrifices.

Jesus Is Greater as the New and Living Way
(Hebrews 10:19-13:25)

The author exhorts his readers to appropriate the blessings made possible by Christ's high priesthood (Hebrews 10:19-25). Pondering what Christ has accomplished for his people (Hebrews 10:19-21), he says they should draw near to God's presence (Hebrews 10:22), hold fast to their confession (Hebrews 10:23), consider how to stir up fellow believers to acts of love and good deeds (Hebrews 10:24), never fail to meet regularly with one another, and encourage one another every day (Hebrews 10:25).

In Hebrews 10:26-31, we find the author's fourth warning passage. The strong warning set forth here parallels the statement in 6:4-8. This passage, like the earlier one, exposes the danger of apostasy. The author insists that his readers demonstrate genuine faith by their continued commitment to Christ. Although they have already suffered for their faith, they need to display continued stamina and obedience to God (Hebrews 10:32-39).

Hebrews 11 provides several illustrations of men and women who exemplified the kind of commitment the author has just exhorted his readers to demonstrate. Many refer to this passage as the "Faith Hall of Fame." After describing the meaning of faith (Hebrews 11:1-3), the author recounts great faith exploits of Israel's heroes before the Flood (Hebrews 11:4-7), the faith of Abraham and Sarah (Hebrews 11:8-19), the faith of the subsequent patriarchs (Hebrews 11:20-22), the faith of Moses (Hebrews 11:23-28), the faith of the Exodus generation (Hebrews 11:29-31), and the faith of other servants of God (Hebrews 11:32-38). The author concludes the chapter with the forward-looking nature of faith (Hebrews 11:39-40). Faith celebrates the reality of God's future blessings, grounded in God's promises and therefore certain. This chapter clearly rebukes preachers who promise God's people they will be healthy and wealthy in this present life. The great men and women of faith in this chapter demonstrate the fallacy of any such teaching.

The example of Jesus should encourage readers to persevere in faith (Hebrews 12:1-3). God disciplines those who fail to follow Jesus' example (Hebrews 12:4-13). God's discipline expresses his Fatherly love for his people. God wants his people to pursue peace and holiness (Hebrews 12:14-29). The author illustrates Christian holiness in real-world living by encouraging his readers to love others (Hebrews 13:1-6), to follow the example of godly leaders (Hebrews 13:7-8), to offer Christian sacrifices (Hebrews 13:9-16), to obey one's spiritual leaders (Hebrews 13:17), and to be intercessors (Hebrews 13:18-19).

The book concludes with a request for readers to pay careful attention to this "brief exhortation," a report on Timothy's circumstances, greetings from those who are with the author, and a final blessing (Hebrews 13:20-25).

Living Out the Message of Hebrews

As we consider how to live out the message of Hebrews, we must begin with Jesus. Repeatedly, the author highlights Jesus' superiority. He is superior to the Old Testament prophets, angels, Moses, and Joshua. Jesus' high priesthood is superior to the Aaronic priesthood, and his sacrificial death is superior to every Old Testament sacrifice ever offered. Jesus secures for his people a new and better covenant. How, then, can God's people not love Jesus more obediently, worship him more sincerely, and advance his gospel more boldly?

Christ's person and work should motivate God's people to live godly lives to Christ's glory. Following Jesus will not eliminate difficulties; in fact, difficulties may increase due to persecution.

Yet, faith does not turn back, but by God's grace keeps its eyes on Jesus, the author and finisher of his people's faith.

A deeper understanding of Christ's work as high priest and sacrifice helps us realize the full freedom of our access into the presence of God. Under the old covenant, only the high priest entered God's presence, and then only once a year. As a result of Christ's death, God's people may boldly enter God's presence at any time. Will we take advantage of this privilege? Prayerless saints fail to avail themselves of this tremendous blessing—but God's door always remains open to them.

Finally, chapter 11 provides a striking reminder of the importance of faith. Faith in Christ enables the people of God to live in victory. Victory in Christ does not look like we might imagine. The saints listed in chapter 11 demonstrated their faith by their obedience, and so brought God much glory. Mature faith looks forward to an eternal city whose builder and maker is God (Hebrews 11:10). Chapter 12 teaches us that Jesus is our example for running the race (Hebrews 12:1-3). When we get off course, our heavenly Father lovingly disciplines us so that we run the race rightly (Hebrews 12:4-13). Chapter 13 helps us understand what running the race looks like as the writer exhorts his readers to love and do good to others (Hebrews 13:1-16), obey their leaders (Hebrews 13:17), and pray (Hebrews 13:18).

20

James

Saving Faith Works

JAMES IS THE PROVERBS of the New Testament. The author deals with the everyday issues of living the Christian life: trials, temptation, showing favoritism, the importance of words, the struggle with worldliness, and many other relevant topics.

The Big Picture

Several men in the New Testament are called James, although overwhelming consensus declares the author of this book to be James, the half-brother of Jesus, a leading figure in the early church. Although James did not follow his brother before the Crucifixion, he received a special Resurrection appearance from Jesus that changed his life (1 Corinthians 15:7). James later became the leader of the Jerusalem church. The book named for him is normally thought to be the earliest of the Christian writings, probably written in the mid-40s. The evidence for this dating is the distinctive Jewish flavor of the book and the reference to the recipients as the twelve tribes dispersed abroad. The book reflects a simple church structure consisting of teachers (James 3:1) and elders (James 5:14). It does not mention the Jerusalem conference controversy, which may have changed how James expressed himself in the discussion on faith and works.

The book initially had a hard time gaining widespread acceptance, likely because of its practical nature and its lack of extended doctrinal teaching. Another likely reason is the author's failure to mention the Holy Spirit. Eventually, however, the church accepted the book into the Canon.

James probably wrote from Jerusalem or somewhere nearby. His readers apparently were suffering local persecution from their countrymen. James wanted to strengthen their faith and help them know how to live out the Christian life in a hostile setting.

Observe several key themes as you read the book. First, notice James's teaching about the tongue, to which he returns repeatedly. Second, James highlights the dangers of wealth and worldliness, two of Satan's chief strategies in derailing a believer's faith.

Outline

James is not an easy book to outline because the author frequently shifts from topic to topic. Allowing the author's natural flow to unfold as the book progresses may be the best way to outline the book, rather than forcing an unnatural structure upon it.

1. Salutation (James 1:1)

2. Trials, Temptation, and the Word (James 1:2-27)

3. The Sin of Favoritism (James 2:1-13)

4. The Relationship between Faith and Works (James 2:14-26)

5. Controlling the Tongue (James 3:1-12)

6. Wisdom from Above and Wisdom from Below (James 3:13-18)

7. The Wickedness of Worldliness and a Call to Repentance (James 4:1-12)

8. Egotistical Indifference: Planning for the Future without God (James 4:13-17)

9. Misusing Wealth and Abusing the Poor (James 5:1-6)

10. Exhortations to the Suffering (James 5:7-12)

11. The Importance of Prayer in All Circumstances (James 5:13-20)

Digging Into James

Salutation (James 1:1)

The author identifies himself as James, a servant of God and of the Lord Jesus Christ. If this James is indeed the half-brother of Jesus, his refusal to mention his earthly heritage reflects his humility. He says he writes to Jewish Christians scattered abroad. James uses the typical greeting in the Greco-Roman world.

Trials, Temptation, and the Word (James 1:2-27)

James begins by encouraging his suffering readers to endure trials with joy (James 1:2-12), possible only because they know that God uses trials to refine their faith, produce endurance in them, and develop their Christian character (James 1:2-4). James's thought accords with the rest of the New Testament's teaching on the believer's attitude toward trials (Matthew 5:11-12; Acts 5:41; Romans 5:3; 2 Corinthians 7:4; Hebrews 10:34; 1 Peter 1:6).

Believers need God's wisdom to make wise decisions during trying times, so they must pray (James 1:5-8). People tend to make poor decisions when trials cloud their thoughts. Although God makes his wisdom available to his people, it must be sought through prayer (James 1:6-8). They must ask in faith and not divide their loyalties between God and the world. James sets forth two examples of trials: poverty and prosperity (James 1:9-11), both of which carry their own unique difficulties. James concludes his discussion on trials by highlighting the great reward for those who patiently endure suffering, thereby demonstrating their love for God (James 1:12).

James next turns his focus to temptation (James 1:13-18). God is not responsible for temptation (James 1:13-16); temptation comes from within the individual. James uses the imagery of childbirth and fishing to show how temptation works. At this point, he focuses on indwelling sin and does not mention the role Satan plays in temptation. Just as a fish gets drawn off course by the right bait, so believers must beware when Satan entices them with "bait," luring their indwelling sin toward the hook. Lust, sin, and death—that is the order.

James gives a stern warning against deception in verse 16. He does not want his readers to think that God in any way tempts anyone to sin. Rather, God is the source of everything good, especially the gift of the new birth (James 1:17-18).

How can believers navigate the treacherous waters of trials and temptations? Only by practicing the Word of God (James 1:19-27). The passage centers around three commands: hear the Word, receive the Word, practice the Word. A person who hears the Word but doesn't put it into practice lands in real danger. Those who do not obey the Word delude themselves into thinking they are righteous. James concludes the chapter with a description of a follower of true religion: one who controls the tongue, cares for the marginalized, and lives a holy life.

The Sin of Favoritism (James 2:1-13)

Those who have entered a faith relationship with Jesus Christ must not let social distinctions and financial differences determine how they treat others. Favoritism has no place in the Christian life. James offers a warning against it (James 2:1) and provides an illustration of what favoritism looks like (James 2:2-4). In verses 5-13, James expands on the utter sinfulness of favoritism. Favoritism is antithetical to the purpose of God (James 2:5-6), is not in the interest of the believer (James 2:6-7), and is a sin against the law of love (James 2:8-13).

The Relationship between Faith and Works (James 2:14-26)

This is the most controversial passage in the letter. On the surface, James appears to contradict Paul's teaching of justification by faith; but on closer examination, he does not. We will first walk through the passage and then say a few words about the debate.

James first declares that saving faith is no meaningless assertion (James 2:14-17). Individuals can *say* they have faith, but if their lives *show* no evidence of faith, then their confession must be called into question. James illustrates his point by showing how one's lifestyle can contradict one's words (James 2:15-16). James then applies his illustration to the principle under discussion, that faith without the evidence of fruit is dead (James 2:17). Faith is more than merely the confession of a creed. The demons confess that God is one, but they shudder in fear of God.

James then illustrates genuine faith by recalling the lives of Abraham and Rahab, beginning with Abraham (James 2:21-24). In verse 23, James asserts that Scripture was fulfilled in the offering of Isaac. The Scripture quoted (Genesis 15:6) refers to God's declaration of Abraham's righteousness based upon Abraham's faith, many years prior to the offering of Isaac. Years before, God had declared Abraham righteous. Abraham's willingness to sacrifice his son *demonstrated* his righteousness rather than *establishing* it.

James next uses Rahab to illustrate that works reveal genuine faith (James 2:25). In their backgrounds, Rahab and Abraham were as far apart as two people could be—and yet, James selects her as an example of obedient faith (as does the author of Hebrews). The conclusion is clear: Faith is revealed by works (James 2:26).

Paul and James do not contradict one another, but they do differ in their use of the terms "works" and "faith." Paul condemns works as a means of gaining salvation. James uses works as an evidence of salvation. Paul uses the term "faith" to refer to personal trust and commitment to Christ as Savior and Lord. James uses the term "faith" to mean mere intellectual assent to truth, like demons asserting the truth of monotheism.

Controlling the Tongue (James 3:1-12)

Controlling the tongue provides an example of the outworking of genuine faith. Those who teach the Word must be very careful what they teach because their words influence how others live (James 3:1). The impact of the words one speaks can direct their entire lives (James 3:2-5). James illustrates the power of the tongue by means of three vivid figures: a bit in a horse's mouth, a rudder of a ship, and a spark of fire. In the final metaphor, an uncontrolled tongue is like a forest fire bringing destruction and devastation. The mention of a fire consuming a forest leads James to discuss the malicious, destructive nature of the tongue. James makes his point by stacking up metaphors to demonstrate the great damage a person can bring when they do not control their mouths (James 3:6-8), which should never be true of believers (James 3:9-12).

Wisdom from Above and Wisdom from Below (James 3:13-18)

The words one uses reflect the wisdom that fills one's mind. This wisdom comes either from heaven above (James 3:13, 17-18) or from hell below (James 3:14-16).

The Wickedness of Worldliness and a Call to Repentance (James 4:1-12)

We should not disassociate this passage from James's discussion of wisdom. We can see the whole passage as a fairly complete treatment of a life that follows worldly wisdom rather than heavenly wisdom. Worldly wisdom gets expressed in its choice of worldly pleasure as the chief pursuit of life (James 4:1-10), characterized by "quarrels and fights" (James 4:1-2), the destruction of effective prayer (James 4:3), and a life repugnant to God (James 4:4-6). Those who choose this lifestyle commit spiritual adultery against God and choose to be a friend of the world rather than a friend of God. A jealous God, however, will not tolerate rivals.

Repentance is the appropriate response for those who fall into such worldliness (James 4:7-10). Derogatory speech toward fellow believers provides another example of a spirit of worldliness (James 4:11-12). In one sense, these two verses reflect a life devoid of humility, which James calls for in the previous verses. When someone speaks disparagingly against another, they put their sinful choice above obedience to God's Word, which forbids such speech.

Egotistical Indifference: Planning for the Future without God (James 4:13-17)

Planning for one's future without seeking God provides another example of worldly thinking. God has plans for his people, and they should seek his guidance in making major decisions in life. To fail to seek God about these decisions implies we are wise enough in ourselves to make these decisions without him.

Misusing Wealth and Abusing the Poor (James 5:1-6)

Here James speaks something like an Old Testament prophet. He focuses on the wealthy landowners who abused the poor laborers who worked for them. James clearly exposes a range of sins, including exploitation of poor laborers, injustice, luxurious and extravagant living at the expense of the poor, and physical violence. God's judgment on these sins is certain.

Exhortations to the Suffering (James 5:7-12)

Here James emphasizes patience and endurance. He encourages his readers to suffer patiently, for one day the Lord will return (James 5:7-11). James provides several examples of suffering well: the farmer (James 5:7), the prophets (James 5:10), and Job (James 5:11). James returns to the topic of speech in 5:12, a recurring theme (James 1:19, 26; 3:1-12; 4:11, 13; 5:9). Honesty should characterize the believer's speech.

JOURNEY THROUGH THE NEW TESTAMENT

The Importance of Prayer in All Circumstances
(James 5:13-20)

Prayer and praise should characterize a believer's life in times of suffering (James 5:13), in times of joy (James 5:13), and in times of sickness (James 5:14-15). The experience of Elijah should provide an incentive to pray (James 5:16-18). Prayer is especially important in ministry to backsliders (James 5:19-20).

Living Out the Message of James

Since James touches on so many important topics, I will select two for special attention.

First, consider the tongue. Jesus made clear that our words reflect our hearts (Matthew 12:34). Our words can build others up or tear them down. Our words have a big influence on the course of our lives. Though the tongue is small, so is a bit in the mouth of a horse, or a rudder that controls a ship. This small part of the body can do great damage to ourselves and others. Our words can be like a tiny spark that sets a forest (or a life) aflame. Maturing believers must gain control of the tongue. We must not sing praises to God at church and then criticize our Sunday school teacher on the way home. Getting control of the tongue requires determination to put sin to death. As we do, we glorify God and edify those around us.

Second, James urges us to respond appropriately to trials. He begins his letter with this topic. He does not tell us to consider all trying things as joy; that would require us to pretend that trials are neither difficult nor hard. We do not rejoice in the trials, but in how God uses them for our good. He uses them to purify our faith, develop our character, and teach us how to live with endurance. Growth in sanctification requires knowing how to suffer well. God never wastes our trials, nor should we.

21

1 Peter

Hope for a Suffering Pilgrim People

FIRST PETER IS WRITTEN to those who know about suffering. We find the words *trials*, *suffering*, or *persecution* in every chapter of the book. The persecution is probably localized rather than an official governmental persecution, but whether they suffer at the hands of fellow countrymen or experience the heartache of living in a fallen world, God's people must learn how to suffer well. As in all good things, Jesus is our example. Over and over in this epistle, Peter points to Jesus to teach his readers how to suffer well.

The Big Picture

Most evangelical scholars believe the author is Peter the apostle. The author claims to be "Peter, an apostle of Jesus Christ" (1 Peter 1:1). Second Peter appears to refer to the first letter (2 Peter 3:1). Early church testimony of Peter's authorship is strong. Peter appears to have used Silas as his secretary (1 Peter 5:12).

We know quite a bit about Peter from the Gospels. After Jesus, the Gospels mention Peter by name more than any other person. Peter was one of Jesus' first followers (Mark 1:16-20). Along with James and John, Peter became one of Jesus' inner circle. Peter must have had a big personality because he became the spokesperson for the Twelve (Mark 8:29; John 6:68). Matthew describes Peter walking briefly on the Sea of Galilee (Matthew 14:28-33). Peter impulsively pronounced his willingness to die for Jesus in the upper room, but Jesus told him he would deny him three times (John 13:37-38). Jesus predicted that Peter would one day die for him by crucifixion (John 21:18-19). Early church tradition reports Peter did die by crucifixion in Rome under Nero. After Jesus' resurrection, Peter became a key figure in the early church (Acts 1–12). Following Peter's sermon on the Day of Pentecost, three thousand

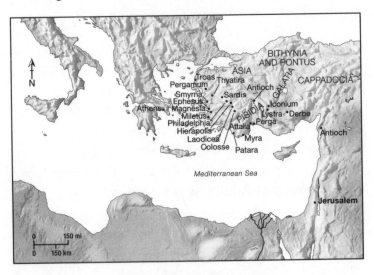

The Churches of Peter's Letter

people came to saving faith (Acts 2:41). After a second sermon, two thousand more were saved (Acts 4:4). Peter did not waste his life dwelling on his past failures, but instead seized the opportunities the Lord provided to serve Jesus well.

The comment in 1 Peter 5:13, "Your sister church here in Babylon sends you greetings," suggests Peter wrote from Rome, cryptically referred to as Babylon. Almost surely he wrote the letter in AD 62–63, after Paul's release from his first Roman imprisonment. If Paul had been imprisoned while Peter was in Rome, almost certainly Peter would have mentioned him. Peter's intended audience appears to be primarily Gentile Christians, with a minority of Jewish Christians (1 Peter 1:18; 2:10; 4:3). First Peter 1:1 lists five locations, all Roman provinces in Asia Minor (modern-day Turkey). Peter wrote the letter because his readers were being persecuted for their faith (1 Peter 1:6; 3:13-17; 4:12-19). Therefore, Peter wanted to encourage them to be gospel witnesses to a hostile world by demonstrating Christlikeness in their suffering.

As you read 1 Peter, notice the significant number of Old Testament references and allusions in the book. Keep an eye out for references to persecution and suffering, and make sure to notice the repeated references to Jesus throughout the book. Finally, take note of the way Peter describes God's people.

Outline

1. Salutation (1 Peter 1:1-2)

2. A Prayer of Thanksgiving for Our Salvation (1 Peter 1:3-12)

3. Exhortations to Obedient Living (1 Peter 1:13–3:12)

4. Encouragement to a Suffering People (1 Peter 3:13–5:11)

5. Final Greetings (1 Peter 5:12-14)

Digging Into 1 Peter

Salutation (1 Peter 1:1-2)

Peter addresses this letter to churches spread throughout Asia Minor, reminding them of their salvation. Although people may reject them, God chose these believers for salvation through the work of the Father, Son, and Holy Spirit. Though they have a lofty spiritual position as "God's chosen people," from an earthly perspective they are "foreigners" and "temporary residents." In other words, they are God's people, temporarily living in a foreign land that is not their eternal home.

A Prayer of Thanksgiving for our Salvation (1 Peter 1:3-12)

The body of the epistle begins with thanksgiving to God. Peter's heart overflows with love and a deep understanding of the greatness of his salvation. This passage functions as a hymn of praise, divided into three stanzas: praise to God for the blessings of the new birth (1 Peter 1:3-5), praise to God for joy amid suffering (1 Peter 1:6-9), and praise to God for the greatness of salvation (1 Peter 1:10-12). Peter emphasizes the *future* orientation of the Christian's hope of salvation (cf. 1 Peter 1:13). He uses the metaphor of an inheritance kept safe for believers until the last days, one reason why believers can experience joy while suffering. Hope ("great expectation") characterizes the Christian life and anticipates a future salvation not yet fully revealed.

Exhortations to Obedient Living (1 Peter 1:13-3:12)

With this newfound identity as children of God, believers are to pursue a new way of life (1 Peter 1:14), characterized by hope and holiness (1 Peter 1:13-16), godly fear (1 Peter 1:17-21), and love toward others (1 Peter 1:22). This love follows being born again by the Word of God (1 Peter 1:23).

Peter insists that spiritual growth is a process. Believers must put off sin and instead crave the Scriptures (1 Peter 2:1-3). Spiritual growth is not merely an individual pursuit but involves being a part of a community of faith (1 Peter 2:4-10). Peter's readers are God's people and are to serve him as missionaries, declaring his mighty acts among the nations.

Peter shifts gears at this point and focuses on the outworking of faith in Christ in a sinful world. He calls believers temporary residents and foreigners in this world (1 Peter 2:11) who must fight indwelling sin and seek to live in godly ways before a pagan world (1 Peter 2:11-12).

What does it look like to live in a godly way before a watching world? Peter explains in 2:13–3:12. Christian citizens should live in submission to governmental authorities (1 Peter 2:13-17). Christian slaves should work hard and live in submission to their masters (1 Peter 2:18-25), following the example of Jesus as they suffer unjustly. Jesus willingly suffered unjust treatment but refused to retaliate. Jesus' death secured the forgiveness of our sins (1 Peter 2:21-25).

Peter returns to the responsibilities of believers living in a fallen world. Wives should be characterized by submission, purity, and reverence (1 Peter 3:1-6). The call to husbands is equally important, although briefer (1 Peter 3:7). Husbands are to honor their wives and live with them in an understanding way. If a Christian husband fails to love his wife in this way, his prayers will be hindered. God takes seriously a husband's responsibility to his wife! The final paragraph summarizes this larger section that began at 2:11. The Lord requires believers to pursue righteousness and avoid wickedness, especially by treating others with kindness (1 Peter 3:8-12).

Encouragement to a Suffering People (1 Peter 3:13–5:11)

God calls Christians to endure suffering and hardship (1 Peter 3:13-17), but we must suffer for doing good rather than evil. Jesus' death on the cross provides the perfect example of suffering unjustly (1 Peter 3:18-22). This passage is one of the most difficult passages to interpret in 1 Peter. The main point here is that Jesus gives us an example of suffering well for God's glory. Jesus died for the sins of others. His suffering and death resulted in victory and vindication. Jesus declared his victory and Satan's doom to fallen angels at his ascension (1 Peter 3:22). Peter compares Noah's flood to baptism, which does not save, but gives us a picture of God's cleansing of the believer at salvation (1 Peter 3:21).

Since Christ suffered for believers and has left them an example of how to suffer well, they should prepare themselves to suffer (1 Peter 4:1-6). Christians must not waste their lives pursuing fleshly desires but instead must seek to do God's will (1 Peter 4:3-6). The nearness of Christ's return should motivate believers to pray, love one another, and diligently use their spiritual gifts (1 Peter 4:7-11). Peter does not want his readers' sufferings to surprise them (1 Peter 4:12). They should rejoice because their suffering for Christ is a blessing and identifies them as his followers (1 Peter 4:13-19).

Peter then provides a series of exhortations, beginning with elders (1 Peter 5:1-4) and then all believers (1 Peter 5:5-11). Elders must lead their flock through suffering. Peter describes pastoral ministry through three sets of contrasts: not grudgingly, but willingly; not for monetary gain, but a desire to serve; and not in a domineering manner, but leading by example. Peter wants all believers to live humbly with one another and to watch for the devil, a roaring lion (1 Peter 5:5-9). Peter reminds them of God's promise of eternal glory (1 Peter 5:10-11).

Final Greetings (1 Peter 5:12-14)

Peter concludes the letter by urging his readers to stand firm in God's grace. Even in persecution and suffering, the Christian must stand firm in the faith given through Jesus Christ.

Living Out the Message of 1 Peter

Christians are aliens and strangers in a foreign land. This world is not their home, and so it is a dangerous place because of its temptations to sin, painful trials, and persecutions. Because believers live in a fallen world, they should expect much suffering. Therefore, believers must know how to suffer well. *Hope* is an important word (1 Peter 1:3, 13, 21; 3:15), especially since hopelessness permeated the ancient world. Christian hope is a confident expectation that God will do what he has promised. If believers are to endure suffering, they must keep their hope focused on God and his promises.

Furthermore, if believers are to suffer well, they must follow in the footsteps of Jesus (1 Peter 2:21-25; 3:18-22; 4:1-2; 5:1). Jesus gives us the greatest example of unjust suffering the world has ever known. He died for sinners to bring them to God (1 Peter 2:24-25; 3:18). When others reviled him, he did not revile them; and while suffering, he uttered no threats (1 Peter 2:23), but entrusted his life into God's hands. Though following Jesus' example in suffering is no easy task, God has not left us to suffer all alone. God's Spirit indwells all believers, empowering them to endure suffering well.

Finally, remember that God does not waste our sufferings, but uses them to conform us into Christ's image. God also uses our sufferings as a witness to the world. People will stand in amazement as Christians suffer in a way that glorifies God. Suffering also reminds us that we are not home yet.

22

2 Peter

Beware of False Teachers

THE CHURCH IN Peter's day, as in our own, finds itself endangered by false teachers. These teachers do not come with signs around their necks identifying them as heretics. False teachers often have charismatic personalities and persuasive speaking skills. They may even have a large following on social media. Unless believers pay close attention, they can be swept away with these false teachers' adoring followers. Peter had similar concerns for the churches to which he wrote.

Commentator Michael Green catches the feel of 2 Peter (and Jude) when he writes, "We can hardly maintain that 2 Peter and Jude, written as they were to meet problems very [much] like our own, have nothing to teach us. So long as sin needs to be exposed, so long as man needs to be reminded that persistent wrongdoing ends in ruin, that lust is self-defeating, that intellectualism devoid of love is a barren thing, and that Christian theology has no right to outrun 'the faith once delivered to the saints,' these Epistles will remain uncomfortably, burningly relevant."[12]

The Big Picture

Scholars widely dispute the authorship of 2 Peter, although the book claims to be written by Peter: "This letter is from Simon Peter, a slave and apostle of Jesus Christ" (2 Peter 1:1). The author also asserts personal reflections of his time with Jesus:

> And it is only right that I should keep on reminding you as long as I live. For our Lord Jesus Christ has shown me that I must soon leave this earthly life, so I will work hard to make sure you always remember these things after I am gone.
>
> For we were not making up clever stories when we told you about the powerful coming of our Lord Jesus Christ. We saw his majestic splendor with our own eyes.
>
> 2 PETER 1:13-16

Those who deny Peter's authorship point to several issues, the first having to do with differences in the writing style between 1 and 2 Peter. A second concern involves the difficult time the book had being accepted into the Canon (although ultimately it was accepted). A third issue involves the reference to Paul's letters in 3:15-16, which suggests the author refers to a collection of Pauline letters, although this type of collection did not take place during Peter's lifetime.

Though a full defense of Peter's authorship is beyond the scope of this work, a few comments are in order. First, the fact remains that the letter does claim to be written by Peter. Second, we know that Silas helped Peter to write his first letter (1 Peter 5:12), which may account for some stylistic differences between the two letters. Third, the comments made by the author regarding his personal times with Christ are either outright lies or genuine. It is hard to conceive of an author insisting on such high ethical standards and yet making such a falsehood. Fourth, the author's reference to a previous letter fits well with both letters being written by the same person. Finally, we should not discount the possibility that some of Paul's earliest letters may have circulated at an early date. All these points argue in favor of accepting Peter as the author.

Peter probably wrote this letter between AD 65 and 68. Early church tradition indicates Peter died during the Neronian persecution of Christians in Rome in the mid to late 60s. Therefore, Peter likely wrote this letter from Rome, shortly before his execution.

Peter writes to the same churches he addressed in his first letter: "This is my second letter to you, dear friends, and in both of them I have tried to stimulate your wholesome thinking and refresh your memory" (2 Peter 3:1). While the readers of Peter's first letter suffered persecution from without, in this letter they are in danger from false teachers within (seen by an abundance of warnings throughout the letter). Therefore, Peter wrote this letter because of his deep concern for the spiritual well-being of his readers, warning them of the encroaching danger of false teaching.

Peter wrote, first, to encourage his readers to grow spiritually so that they could withstand the assault of false teachers (2 Peter 1). Second, Peter gives extensive teaching on the character of the heretical teachers and their dangerous doctrine (2 Peter 2). Third, Peter reminds them that this life is not all there is. A new heaven and a new earth are coming after Jesus returns (2 Peter 3).

Before we dig into the content of 2 Peter, we need to consider the letter's relationship to the book of Jude. Second Peter and Jude are very similar, as both focus on the danger of heretical teachers. Peter and Jude also approach the heretical teachers and their false teaching in comparable ways. The closeness of wording in certain passages suggests a literary relationship between the two (e.g., compare Jude 1:4, 6-9, 12, 18 with 2 Peter 2:1, 3-4, 6, 10-11, 13, 17). Whether one author borrowed from the other, or they both used a common source, is impossible to know. At best, both authors clearly felt compelled to help their readers to identify heretical teachers.

As you read 2 Peter, observe Peter's strong words about false teachers. Contrary to our day, when we hear that we should treat every voice as equal, Peter understood the danger of false teaching and refused to treat it lightly. In the opening chapter, Peter lets his readers know that the antidote to heresy is a vibrant spiritual life. Finally, notice what Peter teaches about Christ's second coming and the end of the age.

Outline

A broad outline of 2 Peter breaks the book down into three large sections bracketed on each side by an introduction and conclusion.

1. Introduction (2 Peter 1:1-2)

2. An Exhortation to Spiritual Maturity (2 Peter 1:3-21)

3. A Warning against Heretical Teachers (2 Peter 2:1-22)

4. The Coming Day of the Lord (2 Peter 3:1-16)

5. Concluding Exhortations (2 Peter 3:17-18)

Digging Into 2 Peter

Introduction (2 Peter 1:1-2)

Peter's introduction echoes other New Testament introductions, except that he affirms the deity of Jesus: "Jesus Christ, our God and Savior." He also highlights the importance of growing in one's knowledge of God the Father and Jesus our Lord.

An Exhortation to Spiritual Maturity (2 Peter 1:3-21)

Peter reminds his readers that God has provided all they need for them to grow in the grace and knowledge of Jesus Christ. Peter lists the qualities they should seek to develop in verses 5-7. Christians who fail to develop these qualities forget the horror from which God has saved them (2 Peter 1:8-9). Spiritual fruitfulness provides evidence of God's election (2 Peter 1:10-11).

Peter knows that his life is nearing its end, so he desires to remind his readers how they ought to live (2 Peter 1:12-15). He had been an eyewitness of the ministry of Jesus. The example he provides summarizes what took place on the Mount of Transfiguration (2 Peter 1:16-18). Peter affirms the truthfulness of Scripture (2 Peter 1:19-21). His apostolic testimony and Scripture's teaching provide sure guides for his readers. In verse 21, Peter affirms the inspiration of Scripture.

A Warning against Heretical Teachers (2 Peter 2:1-22)

Just as false prophets plagued Israel's past, so false teachers would seek to undermine the church. Their coming was foretold. These heretical teachers will teach destructive heresy, deny Christ's lordship, engage in sexual immorality, and have a taste for greed (2 Peter 2:1-3). Peter uses examples from Genesis to demonstrate God's willingness to judge ungodliness: fallen angels

(Genesis 6:1-4), the Flood in Noah's day (Genesis 7:17-23), and Sodom and Gomorrah (Genesis 19:23-29). At the same time, God delivered Noah and his family from the Flood (Genesis 7:13-16) and Lot from the judgment of Sodom and Gomorrah (Genesis 19:29). In the same way, God can rescue Peter's readers from the false teachers endangering them (2 Peter 2:4-10). Peter provides a helpful list of characteristics and practices to help his readers identify heretical teachers:

- They are proud and arrogant, scoffing at supernatural beings (2 Peter 2:10-11).
- They are like wild animals (2 Peter 2:12).
- They are self-indulgent and deceptive (2 Peter 2:13).
- They are greedy (2 Peter 2:14).
- They have forsaken the truth and gone astray like Balaam (2 Peter 2:15-16).
- Their teaching overflows with empty promises and boastful words (2 Peter 2:17-19).
- Given time, their true character eventually emerges (2 Peter 2:20-22).

The Coming Day of the Lord (2 Peter 3:1-16)

Peter reminds his readers that in the last days scoffers will appear, denying the second coming of Jesus (2 Peter 3:1-4). Peter replies to these scoffers in verses 5-10. God intervened in history at Creation (2 Peter 3:5) and again at the Flood (2 Peter 3:6). God will intervene once more in judgment at the end of history (2 Peter 3:7). Peter explains God's apparent delay of Christ's return (2 Peter 3:8-10). The Lord's perspective on time differs a great deal from our perspective on time, and in fact, the Lord's delay demonstrates his gracious forbearance. Still, God's cosmic judgment will come.

Once again, Peter urges his readers to live a godly life as they reflect on the coming of a new heaven and a new earth (2 Peter 3:11-13). As believers await that day, they must pursue godliness (2 Peter 3:14-16).

Concluding Exhortations (2 Peter 3:17-18)

These closing comments are likely the final words written by the great apostle before his martyrdom. Peter appeals to his readers not to be caught off guard or surprised by the presence of heretical teachers. Instead, they should seek to grow in the grace and knowledge of our Lord Jesus Christ.

Living Out the Message of 2 Peter

Theological error and moral error go together, and both are serious matters. Peter speaks with a forthrightness that makes many contemporary people uncomfortable. He understood that bad doctrine results in bad living. If one believes a false gospel, all hope is lost. If believers get led astray by heresy, they will make poor moral choices. False teachers often use the "right" words but assign alternate meanings to them. Growing into Christlikeness requires sound doctrine.

On the one hand, we need not doubt God's intention to judge heretical teachers. Peter points to the fallen angels, the sinful world of Noah's day, and Sodom and Gomorrah to remind us of God's willingness to judge evil. On the other hand, the examples of Noah and Lot show us that we need not fear that God will forget to give his people the help they need to keep from succumbing to heresy. Conformity to Christ requires effort on the part of God's people. Believers must know the truth, and by God's grace, live out that truth. The Spirit of God and the Word of God work together in the believer's sanctification. God has provided the qualities listed in 2 Peter 1:5-7 to enable believers to live in a godly way—and each of those qualities should land high on the priority list of every believer in every age.

23

1, 2, and 3 John

Assurance of Salvation

FIRST JOHN HAS had a huge impact far beyond its size. Many believers through the ages have turned to 1 John when struggling with assurance of salvation and have found within its pages both comfort and reason for concern. All three letters are relevant to the modern era. Just as the contemporary church is under attack from all sides, so the churches to which John wrote also were under assault. The references to false teachers and people abandoning the faith and leaving the church show the further relevance of these books.

The Big Picture

From the earliest days of the post-apostolic church, these letters have been attributed to John the apostle. Their similarities to the fourth Gospel point in the same direction. The letters and the Gospel have a common vocabulary and address similar topics, such as love and hate, truth and error, and light and darkness. The author of 1 John identifies himself as an eyewitness of the ministry of Jesus (1 John 1:1, 3; 4:14; 5:6-7). The author of the second and third letters identifies himself as "the elder" (2 John 1:1; 3 John 1:1). Whether he uses the term as a reference to his age, or a title, or possibly both, is impossible to know. There does not seem to be any good reason for denying Johannine authorship of all three letters.

The apostle John wrote 1 John to combat false teaching endangering the church. Some in these churches had already abandoned the faith and left the church (1 John 2:18-19, 26-27). John uses strong words to denounce the heretical teachers, referring to them as "false prophets" (1 John 4:1), "antichrists" (1 John 2:18; 4:3), and "deceivers" (2 John 1:7).

John provides key insights into the false teachers' heretical teaching. They had a defective Christology that rejected Jesus' true humanity (1 John 2:22-23; 4:2, 15; 2 John 1:7, 9), reminiscent of a type of heretical teaching associated with second-century Gnosticism. Since John wrote before the full flowering of Gnosticism, he likely fought some form of incipient Gnosticism. In addition, these false teachers denied the reality of sin and its effects on them (1 John 1:6-10; 3:4-10).

John wrote 2 John for reasons similar to those that prompted the writing of 1 John, as evidenced by the repeated use of the words *truth* and *love*.

Third John also has a setting of conflict. The apostle wrote to warn the church against the undue influence of Diotrephes.

John states three purposes in writing 1 John. First, "We proclaim to you what we ourselves have actually seen and heard so that you may have fellowship with us. And our fellowship is with the Father and with his Son, Jesus Christ. We are writing these things so that you may fully share our joy" (1 John 1:3-4). Second, "I have written this to you who believe in the name of the Son of God, so that you may know you have eternal life" (1 John 5:13). Third, he writes to combat heretical teaching, which occupies a prominent place throughout the book.

First John is famous for its three "tests" of faith. While these tests have helped struggling believers gain a sense of assurance of their salvation, they have helped others to understand they did not really know Jesus as Savior. John repeats these three tests throughout 1 John. The first test is doctrinal: Christians must believe that Jesus Christ has come in the flesh (4:1-3). The second test focuses on character (holiness): Those who belong to Christ must seek to obey him (1 John 2:29). The third test highlights a believer's genuine love for fellow believers (1 John 3:11).

John wrote 2 John to warn against showing hospitality to false teachers (2 John 1:10), even though John clearly wanted his readers to demonstrate kindness and hospitality to fellow believers.

In 3 John, the apostle warns about the undue influence of Diotrephes, who opposed the apostle. John pointed to Diotrephes's self-serving attitude and desire to gain control of the church.

We cannot know for certain either the place of writing or the dating of these letters. Tradition says John spent the latter part of his life in Asia, associated with the church at Ephesus (Revelation 2:1-7). John likely wrote all three letters from Ephesus. If John wrote his Gospel first, then he wrote the letters in the early 90s.

First John lacks any formal introduction that would identify his intended audience. This lack of a specific addressee may suggest he wrote the letter to churches in and around the city of Ephesus. Second John is addressed "to the chosen lady and to her children" (2 John 1:1), almost certainly not a reference to a specific person, but to a church ("chosen lady") and its members ("children").

Third John is addressed specifically to Gaius, but the letter also appears to have been intended for congregational reading.

Outline: 1 John

From one perspective, 1 John is not a difficult book, with its straightforward message. From another perspective, 1 John is a very difficult book to outline because John repeats his themes. In addition, sometimes he quickly changes topics. The following cumbersome outline nevertheless catches the flow of John's thought.

1. Prologue: The Word of Life (1 John 1:1-4)

2. A Call to Obedience (1 John 1:5–2:6)

3. A Call to Christian Love (1 John 2:7-17)

4. Beware of Antichrists (1 John 2:18-19)

5. A Call to Right Belief (1 John 2:20-27)

6. Another Call to Obedience (1 John 2:28–3:10)

7. Another Call to Christian Love (1 John 3:11-24)

8. Another Call to Right Belief (1 John 4:1-6)

9. Another Call to Christian Love (1 John 4:7-12)

10. Another Call to Right Belief and Love (1 John 4:13-21)

11. The Fundamental Relationship between Love, Obedience, and Belief (1 John 5:1-5)

12. Another Call to Belief in Jesus (1 John 5:6-12)

13. Concluding Remarks (1 John 5:13-21)

Digging Into 1 John

Prologue: The Word of Life (1 John 1:1-4)

John does not begin his letter in typical epistolary style. Instead, he opens with a prologue affirming the incarnation of Jesus Christ. Here John emphasizes the Word of Life's preexistence, his incarnation, and the apostles' interaction with him. John also wrote so his readers could experience genuine joy (1 John 1:4).

A Call to Obedience (1 John 1:5-2:6)

Fellowship with God characterizes the Christian life. Fellowship with God must accord with God's character (1 John 1:5-7) and Christ's work (1 John 2:1-2). This section has three important "if we say . . ." clauses, which introduce three false assertions made by John's opponents. At the heart of the false assertions lies the claim that sin does not truly affect a person (1 John 1:6, 8, 10). John replies forcefully to these spurious claims (1 John 1:7, 9; 2:1). Those who make such claims show themselves to be unbelievers (1 John 1:10). One cannot enjoy fellowship with God apart from obedience to God's commands (1 John 2:3-6). John makes clear that those who know God will obey him. Those who claim to know God but live in disobedience make it obvious they do not know God.

A Call to Christian Love (1 John 2:7-17)

John continues with the theme of obedience, but now relating it to love. Those who know God demonstrate their knowledge by loving their fellow believers (1 John 2:7-8). Those who claim to live in the light but hate others reveal they do not know God (1 John 2:9-11). A genuine love of others indicates that someone knows God. Though the importance of love is not novel to John or his readers, love takes on a fresh, new meaning in the example of Jesus. Christians must love one another but should not love the world (1 John 2:15-17), a seductive mistress. The apostle clarifies here what he means by *world* (1 John 2:16). Love for the world and love for God are mutually exclusive.

Beware of Antichrists (1 John 2:18-19)

John warns his spiritual children that the Antichrist is coming and that many antichrists already have appeared. Notice John's use of the singular, "the Antichrist is coming," and the use of the plural, "many such antichrists have appeared." The singular refers to one personal embodiment of evil to be manifested at the end of the age. The plural refers to those who embody the anti-Christian spirit as forerunners of the final Antichrist. Some have fallen prey to them and have abandoned the faith and left the church. They never really were a part of God's people, or they would have stayed.

A Call to Right Belief (1 John 2:20-27)

In contrast to those who have abandoned the church, John's readers are indwelt by God's Spirit and know (believe) the truth. Those who have fallen prey to a heretical Christology deny Jesus' identity (1 John 2:22-23). John urges his readers to remain in the truth and in the fellowship they have with God through Christ. John takes this opportunity to reassure his readers of their eternal security through the indwelling of the Holy Spirit (1 John 2:20-21, 27) and their union with Christ (1 John 2:27).

Another Call to Obedience (1 John 2:28–3:10)

To be God's child is to enjoy a newfound identity, which establishes a new foundation for righteousness and hope. A child of God must not willfully engage in habitual sin (1 John 3:4, 6, 8), but instead practice righteousness. John further characterizes sin as synonymous with the works of the devil himself, the originator of sin (1 John 3:8). Those born again by God's Spirit do not practice willful, habitual, and intentional sin. John has stated already that Christians sin (1 John 1:9; 2:1-2), but he points now to a disposition that takes sin lightly, enjoys engaging in sinful habits, has no remorse over sin, and has no interest in fighting against it.

Another Call to Christian Love (1 John 3:11-24)

John makes four important points about love. First, love is at the heart of the biblical message (1 John 3:11-12). Second, love provides evidence that a person has passed out of spiritual death into newness of life (1 John 3:13-15). Third, the ultimate demonstration of love was the sacrificial death of Christ on the cross. Since Christ willingly laid down his life for us, we should lay down our lives for others (1 John 3:16-18). Fourth, love produces assurance of our standing before God (1 John 3:20-24).

Another Call to Right Belief (1 John 4:1-6)

John now moves to the discernment needed when judging between a false prophet and one speaking from God's Spirit. Believers discern between true and false spirits through a doctrinal test. Does the speaker believe Jesus Christ is the incarnate Son of God?

Another Call to Christian Love (1 John 4:7-12)

John returns to the concept of love. Genuine believers love one another, while those who do not love reveal that they do not know God. Believers must love one another because love is from God (1 John 4:7-8) and God is love (1 John 4:8-10). When Christians love one another, the actions of God's people make visible the invisible God (1 John 4:12).

Another Call to Right Belief and Love (1 John 4:13-21)

John combines two of his three tests in this section: a call to right belief (1 John 4:13-19) and Christian love (1 John 4:20-21). In this section, John confesses Jesus as the Savior of the world (1 John 4:14). Also in his section, John identifies God as love (1 John 4:16).

The Fundamental Relationship between Love, Obedience, and Belief (1 John 5:1-5)

In this section, John ties together his three tests. When individuals believe that Jesus is the Christ, they will love the Father and fellow believers (1 John 5:1-2). If individuals genuinely love the Father, they will obey him and overcome worldliness (1 John 5:2-4). John concludes this section with a final appeal concerning the necessity of faith if believers are to defeat the sin loved by the world.

Another Call to Belief in Jesus (1 John 5:6-12)

As John began his letter with a reference to Jesus' incarnation, so he closes it (1 John 5:6). He battles the heretical teaching that Jesus died as a mere man. John emphasizes that the eternal God was incarnate in Jesus Christ throughout his earthly life. John offers a fourfold testimony to Christ: the witness of the Spirit (1 John 5:8); the witness of the baptism (water) and death (blood) of Christ (1 John 5:8); the witness of the Father (1 John 5:9); and the inward witness of personal experience (1 John 5:10). God testifies that whoever has the Son has eternal life and whoever does not have the Son does not have life (1 John 5:11-12).

Concluding Remarks (1 John 5:13-21)

John's conclusion summarizes some of the main themes of the epistle and helps his readers have assurance of salvation (1 John 5:13). Notice the repeated use of the word *know* throughout this section. When believers have confidence in their relationship with God, they demonstrate their confidence in prayer (1 John 5:14-17). When believers have assurance of salvation, they gain victory over sin (1 John 5:18). Finally, when believers have assurance that they belong to God as his children, they do not fear the devil or the seduction of the world (1 John 5:19-20). The final verse provides an abrupt but appropriate ending to the letter. Believers must stay committed to the one true God and reject idolatry (1 John 5:21).

Living Out the Message of 1 John

First John repeatedly exhorts its readers to pursue correct doctrine. In an age of spiritual vagueness, 1 John clearly preaches the truth and its importance for those who profess Christ. For John, to believe in something false has eternal consequences. Only through God's Word and the Spirit can we properly examine a teaching (1 John 4:1). Those who seek to preach and teach the Word of God rightly will humbly welcome such examination.

Obedience is closely tied to correct belief, whether that obedience is to walk in the light (1 John 1:7), to keep the commands of the Lord (1 John 2:3), or to practice righteousness (1 John 3:7). For

John, to know rightly but to do wrongly has no value. Obedience and right belief go hand in hand in a life pleasing to God. Never do we forsake one for the other.

John also emphasizes fellowship; in fact, he encourages us to dwell on it. Many today claim that one can live a godly life separated from the church. For John, this is not an option. Fellowship helps in many ways. Fellowship with other believers helps battle false doctrines that may spring up in our own thinking or circle of influence. Through fellowship, believers can perfect the love God shows us. And through fellowship, we discover the best way to fight sin, which involves confession of sin to one another.

The church today faces many "antichrists" that threaten the flock. In the face of these hardships, John encourages believers to hold on to right faith, right practice, and right fellowship until the Lord returns.

Outline: 2 John

Second John is a short but powerful letter. Eugene Peterson captures something of the letter's message when he writes, "The two most difficult things to get straight in life are love and God. More often than not, the mess people make of their lives can be traced to failure or stupidity or meanness in one or both of these areas."[13]

1. Introduction (2 John 1:1-3)

2. Exhortations (2 John 1:4-6)

3. Instructions (2 John 1:7-11)

4. Conclusion (2 John 1:12-13)

Digging Into 2 John

Introduction (2 John 1:1-3)

John identifies himself at the outset simply as "the elder." In the opening verses, he greets his readers and offers affirmation and encouragement. He addresses his letter "to the chosen lady and to her children." We should probably understand "the chosen lady" to refer to the church and "her children" to its members. The New Testament commonly personifies the church as a woman (Revelation 19:7). Furthermore, John regularly refers to his readers as "children" (1 John 2:12, 14, 18, 28; 3:1-2, 7, 10, 18). John grounds his love for his spiritual children "in the truth." His tone sounds like an elderly pastor writing to his beloved sheep. In 2 John 1:3, John bestows God's blessings on the congregation. Grace, mercy, and peace all come from God the Father and Lord Jesus Christ. John then makes another reference to truth and love.

Exhortations (2 John 1:4-6)

John commends the church that her members walk in truth. In verses 5-6, John reminds the congregation to love others in the way prescribed by Jesus (2 John 1:6). Believers should ground their love in truth.

Instructions (2 John 1:7-11)

John warns his readers concerning many "deceivers" who refuse to acknowledge the incarnation of Jesus Christ. The church must keep alert for these heretical teachers who have a defective Christology. John speaks of these false teachers as antichrists. The apostle does not want his readers to engage these false teachers in any way that might assist them in their destructive work (2 John 1:10-11). John does not want the church to show these false teachers hospitality because of their diabolical intentions. He does not mean that Christians should not be hospitable, kind, and caring to unbelievers. Nor does John mean that the church should be inhospitable to its own members. He tells them not to offer hospitality to anyone trying to *destroy* the church.

Conclusion (2 John 1:12-13)

Though John wants to write more to his friends, he prefers to wait and speak to them face-to-face, so that their joy may be made full (cf. 1 John 1:4). His final words include a greeting from a sister church. This brief letter sounds a wakeup call. John wants his readers to know the truth, live in obedience to the truth, and defend the truth. John Stott states,

> Our love is not to be so blind as to ignore the views
> and conduct of others. Truth should make our love
> discriminating. . . . On the other hand, we must never
> champion the truth in a harsh or bitter spirit. . . . So
> the Christian fellowship should be marked equally
> by love and truth, and we are to avoid the dangerous
> tendency to extremism, pursuing either at the expense
> of the other. Our love grows soft if it is not strengthened
> by truth, and our truth grows hard if it is not softened
> by love. We need to live according to Scripture which
> commands us both to love each other in the truth and
> to hold the truth in love.[14]

Living Out the Message of 2 John

Second John reminds us of the importance of being people of truth and love. Both are important for a healthy Christian life. Christians must know the truth; God's Word is truth. We must know it, believe it, and obey it. As John says so often in his Gospel and first letter, if we love God, we will obey him. At the same time we must be people of love. The Pharisees knew the truth of God's Word, but they did not obey God's Word and consequently did not love people. God is love, and his people should love like God loves.

Outline: 3 John

1. Introduction (3 John 1:1-4)

2. Affirmation (3 John 1:5-8)

3. A Warning concerning Diotrephes (3 John 1:9-11)

4. A Commendation of Demetrius (3 John 1:12)

5. Conclusion (3 John 1:13-15)

Digging Into 3 John

Introduction (3 John 1:1-4)
Though John addresses the letter to his dear friend Gaius, he wants the letter read to the entire church. The opening line combines the common pair of words in John's writings, love and truth. A report has come to John about Gaius's graciousness to traveling preachers and his progress in the faith.

Affirmation (3 John 1:5-8)
John expands on his friend's kindness to traveling missionaries. As Gaius cares for them, he demonstrates kindness toward Jesus. John's words recall the time Jesus told his followers that a cup of cold water

given in his name is like giving a cup of cold water to him. John urges Gaius and the church to continue to demonstrate kindness to traveling preachers and missionaries as they serve the Lord. These traveling preachers depend on the goodness of God's people.

A Warning concerning Diotrephes (3 John 1:9-11)

As positive as John has sounded to this point, all is not well. He warns his readers about the negative influence of Diotrephes, who has an insatiable desire to be the center of attention and who rejects John's spiritual leadership over the church. The apostle does not fear to confront Diotrephes and will do so in person when he comes. In contrast to Gaius, Diotrephes refuses to care for traveling preachers and forbids others from doing so. The fact that he can put out of the church those who do assist traveling preachers demonstrates his influence, but his behavior demonstrates that he does not know God.

A Commendation of Demetrius (3 John 1:12)

In contrast to Diotrephes, Demetrius, like Gaius, lives the truth, revealing himself as a follower of God. Both men have a reputation and track record of doing good.

Conclusion (3 John 1:13-15)

As with 2 John, the apostle has much more he wants to say to his readers, but he will refrain until he can see them face-to-face. He blesses them with God's peace, much needed considering the trouble caused by Diotrephes. He sends greetings from those with him.

Living Out the Message of 3 John

On the one hand, this brief letter encourages the people of God to treat well those who preach and teach the Word of God, especially missionaries. On the other hand, this letter warns about those who seek to dominate a congregation and keep them from following God's Word. The latter individuals may have strong and charismatic personalities, but their lifestyle does not conform to the truth. The church must resist and reject their influence—not a pleasant task, but crucial for the health and well-being of the church.

This letter also highlights the importance of commending those who live out the truth. John publicly commends both Gaius and Demetrius. In the busyness of life and ministry, we often fail to publicly commend those who do well. Commending others takes time and thought, but it is important in the workplace, the home, and especially the church.

24

Jude

Defend the Faith

SOMETIMES BIG GIFTS come in small packages, as in the book of Jude. The short letter of Jude has a big and powerful message. It has a single laser-beam focus: to warn believers against capitulating to heretical teaching.

The Big Picture

Jude introduces himself as a "slave of Jesus Christ and brother of James" (Jude 1:1). Most scholars agree that the James noted here refers to James the half-brother of Jesus. If true, then Jude was also a half-brother of Jesus (Matthew 13:55; Mark 6:3). Jude's hesitancy to refer to himself as Jesus' half-brother reflects his humility.

Jude gives a straightforward reason for writing: "Ungodly people have wormed their way into your churches, saying that God's marvelous grace allows us to live immoral lives" (Jude 1:4). Jude wants to exhort his readers to "defend the faith" (Jude 1:3). He focuses on the character of the false teachers more than on their doctrine. He describes them as deceptive (Jude 1:4), sexually immoral (Jude 1:4, 8), disregarding authority (Jude 1:8-10), selfish (Jude 1:12), and boastful (Jude 1:16).

Like the other general epistles, Jude does not name the recipients. Similarities to 2 Peter suggest Jude wrote to churches facing comparable dangers. These similarities may indicate the two letters were written around the same time, but we have no way to know for certain. A date in the mid-60s is probable.

Observe three matters as you read the letter. First, notice Jude's fondness for triads. For example, Jude describes his readers as called, loved, and kept safe (Jude 1:1). He wishes mercy, peace, and love for his readers (Jude 1:2). Three times he addresses them as "dear friends" (Jude 1:3, 17, 20). Second, notice his plethora of references to the Old Testament; apparently, his readers knew these Scriptures well. Third, observe Jude's two uses of two nonbiblical documents.

Outline

1. Introduction (Jude 1:1-4)

2. Warnings against False Teachers (Jude 1:5-16)

3. A Call to Faithfulness (Jude 1:17-23)

4. Concluding Doxology (Jude 1:24-25)

Digging Into Jude

Introduction (Jude 1:1-4)

Jude introduces himself in a very humble fashion, as a slave of Jesus and brother of James. Jude's readers are spiritually secure in their relationship with God: called, loved, and kept safe. He prays that they would have an abundance of mercy, peace, and love.

Though Jude wanted to write on the doctrine of salvation, current circumstances require him to change his focus. He urges his readers to defend the truth against heretical teaching. God has entrusted his people with the truth, and they should proclaim it and defend it. Heretical teachers crept into the church and taught that God's grace encouraged sexual promiscuity, thus clearly rejecting Christ's lordship over their lives.

Warnings against False Teachers (Jude 1:5-16)

Jude elaborates on the diabolical character of these heretical teachers. In verses 5-7, he uses three Old Testament examples of God's judgment to inform his readers that these heretical teachers have fallen under the same sentence of judgment.

First, the Lord destroyed those whom he rescued from Egypt but who did not remain faithful to God.

Second, God judged the fallen angels who engaged in sexual immorality with women (see Genesis 6:4).[15]

Third, God sent the fiery judgment that consumed the cities of Sodom and Gomorrah.

In verses 8-10, Jude calls these false teachers blasphemers. He poses three charges against them in verse 8: They are sexually immoral, they reject authority, and they scorn angelic beings. In verse 9, he demonstrates the significance of their blasphemies with a story from the *Assumption of Moses*, an apocryphal book known by his readers. Jude's use of this book merely illustrates the sin of these false teachers, highlighting the magnitude of their arrogant blaspheming. According to the apocryphal account, God sent the angel Michael to bury the body of Moses. When Lucifer tried to claim the body, Michael showed no disrespect, but left the matter in the Lord's hands and said, "The Lord rebuke you!" Jude's quotation from this work does not indicate he considered the book inspired. He used it much like a preacher might use a news article to illustrate a point in a sermon. According to verse 10, their blasphemies go even further. They reject anything they do not understand, and they give themselves to their most base desires.

In verses 11-13, Jude cites three more biblical examples to illustrate these teachers' sinful behavior: Cain, Balaam, and Korah (Jude 1:11). In verses 12-13, Jude shows the danger of their teaching. When they gather with God's people at the Lord's Supper, they are like "dangerous reefs" that shipwreck believers' faith. The heretics are like autumn trees, "doubly dead" and providing no fruit to meet people's deepest needs. They are like "wild waves of the sea," eroding the seashore of people's faith. The false teachers are like "wandering stars" providing no guidance for life.

A Call to Faithfulness (Jude 1:17-23)

Having revealed the true nature of the enemy, Jude encourages his readers to remain faithful. They must remember the previous warnings that false teachers would appear (Jude 1:17-19). These heretics confirm that the church lives in the last days (which began at Jesus' ascension). The false teachers prove that the Holy Spirit does not indwell them because they seek to justify their sinful behavior and attempt to divide the church.

To counter the seductive influence of heretical teachers, the church must disciple believers in the truth, intercede for one another, and wait expectantly for Jesus' return. They must show mercy to those who struggle because of the diabolical influence of the heretics and refuse to give up on those who unwittingly follow them. Helping those caught in sin is a dangerous business, so they must seek to circumspectly help the lost.

Concluding Doxology (Jude 1:24-25)

Jude concludes his brief letter with a stirring reminder of God's faithfulness to his people and gives glory to God.

Living Out the Message of Jude

As with 2 Peter, Jude reminds us of the reality and danger of false teachers. We recognize false teachers by their heterodox doctrine and their ungodly lifestyle. Heretical teachers are dangerous, as shown by the various Old Testament examples Jude uses. The church should not be shaken or surprised by those who defect from the faith; remember that one of Jesus' own disciples became a traitor. Jude reminds us of the crucial importance of discipleship to a healthy church. Pastors must teach their congregations to both know the truth and live it.

25

Revelation

Come, Lord Jesus!

PICTURE IMAGES OF a great red dragon, a beast coming out of the sea, and locusts rising from a bottomless pit, and you might think you landed in a horror film. But all these images come from Revelation, a book filled with grotesque figures and end-time images. These images and the mystery surrounding them explain why many people find Revelation so difficult to read and understand. These same images, however, cause many others to spend much of their time studying Revelation, but little else in the Bible.

We should not ignore the important book of Revelation. The fact that its images seem strange to twenty-first-century Christians means we must work extra hard to understand the book's message.

The Big Picture

Revelation begins with important words about the author: "This is a revelation from Jesus Christ, which God gave him to show his servants the events that must soon take place. He sent an angel to present this revelation to his servant John" (Revelation 1:1). The author calls himself John (Revelation 1:4, 9; 22:8). The simplicity of the author's designation suggests his readers knew him. The most well-known figure by the name of John in the first century is John the apostle. Early church writers place the apostle John in Ephesus at the end of his life and affirm Johannine authorship of Revelation. Those who oppose John's authorship suggest the style differs too much from John's Gospel and letters. The differences can be explained by the diverse types of literature these writings represent. There seems to be no compelling evidence to deny John's authorship of Revelation.

John says that he wrote from Patmos, an island approximately forty miles southwest of Ephesus in the Aegean Sea. John had been exiled there "for preaching the word of God and for my testimony about Jesus" (Revelation 1:9). Scholars debate when John wrote

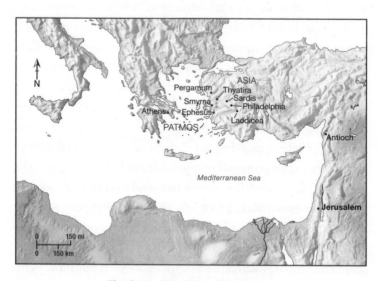

The Seven Churches of Revelation

Revelation. The two most common dates cited are during Nero's reign (mid-60s) or during Domitian's reign (mid to late 90s). The historical details in the book favor a later date. The propagation of emperor worship and the spiritual condition of the seven churches also favor the later date.

The seven letters in chapters 2 and 3 suggest John wrote to these churches in the Roman province of Asia. Though John originally addressed his letters to these specific churches, copies of them spread widely over time.

The book of Revelation contains three differing types of literature, which makes it somewhat difficult to interpret. Though chapters 2 and 3 are epistles, their content and style do not correspond to a typical letter. The author describes the book as a prophecy (Revelation 1:3), and at the same time, the book contains apocalyptic elements (Revelation 1:1). The apocalyptic nature of the book makes it difficult for modern readers to understand. The original readers understood much better than we do the images used throughout the book. Good commentaries on Revelation can help readers understand the author's use of these unfamiliar images.

As you read Revelation, notice God's control of the events taking place in both heaven and on earth. Also, notice that Revelation portrays Jesus in ways that affirm his divinity. Both God the Father and Jesus Christ, for example, are called "the Alpha and the Omega" (Revelation 1:8; 22:13), and both God the Father and Jesus Christ are worshiped by angels in heaven (Revelation 4–5). Also notice that Revelation consistently highlights Christ's victory on the cross (Revelation 1:4-6; 5:6, 9; 12:11; 19:13).

Interpreters tend to take one of four major approaches to the book Revelation. Though the following descriptions are overly simplistic, they do summarize the essence of each position.

The *idealist* approach understands the images of Revelation as symbols that represent timeless truths—the victory of good over evil, for example. This approach does not understand Revelation as a guide to specific end-time events.

The *preterist* interpretation limits the meaning of the book primarily to its original hearers, suggesting the images represent only first-century subjects, such as Caesar, Rome, and Rome's persecution of first-century Christians. From this perspective, the book intends to encourage readers to remain faithful to Jesus while waiting for God to deliver them into his eternal Kingdom.

The *historicist* approach understands the book as a historical timeline from the first century on. The churches in chapters 2–3, for example, depict seven periods of church history. The Reformers especially favored this position, as they understood the Antichrist to be the pope.

The *futurist* position understands much of Revelation to be a window to the end of time. Most of the book's images symbolize the people and events that will play key roles in the final drama of world history. The futurist position has two main variations. *Dispensational* futurists believe all of chapters 4–22 will be fulfilled in the final days of history. A *modified* futurist approach holds that some of the events in chapters 4–22 have occurred already, while others will occur before the end. Though each of these approaches to Revelation provides helpful insight into the book, we will take the modified futurist position.

As you read Revelation, try to grasp the big picture of each chapter before getting into minute details. Many students of the book give up on reading Revelation because they get bogged down in those details. Though details are certainly important, attempt to grasp the big picture of each chapter first, and then return later to dig into the details. The following examination will focus on the big picture of each chapter.

Outline

Outlines of Revelation vary, depending on one's interpretative approach. The following outline seeks to follow the literary structure of the book.

1. Introduction (Revelation 1:1-20)

2. Seven Letters to Seven Churches (Revelation 2:1–3:22)

3. Worship in the Courts of Heaven (Revelation 4:1–5:14)

4. The Seven Seals (Revelation 6:1–8:5)

5. The Seven Trumpets (Revelation 8:6–11:19)

6. Behind the Scenes of the Great War (Revelation 12:1–14:20)

7. The Seven Bowls (Revelation 15:1–16:21)

8. The Fall of Babylon the Great (Revelation 17:1–19:10)

9. Seven Final Events and the Triumph of God (Revelation 19:11–22:5)

10. Conclusion (Revelation 22:6-21)

Digging Into Revelation

Introduction (Revelation 1:1-20)

The first chapter falls into three sections: an introduction (Revelation 1:1-3); a greeting (Revelation 1:4-8); and a vision of the glorified Christ (Revelation 1:9-20). Revelation 1:7 announces the main theme of the book:

> Look! He comes with the clouds of heaven.
>   And everyone will see him—
>   even those who pierced him.
> And all the nations of the world
>   will mourn for him.
> Yes! Amen!

John's vision of the glorified Christ reminds the reader of the importance of grasping the overall meaning of an image rather than getting bogged down in debatable details (Revelation 1:12-16). The vision is meant to encourage the churches that their Savior, the glorified Lord, walks among the churches.

Seven Letters to Seven Churches (Revelation 2:1–3:22)

These chapters reproduce seven letters to seven churches located in Asia Minor. These letters reveal the great dangers facing these churches: persecution, heretical teaching, and moral compromise. The letters encourage the churches to endure persecution, confront and reject heresy, and live holy, God-honoring lives.

Worship in the Courts of Heaven (Revelation 4:1–5:14)

Revelation 4 and 5 present visions of worship in heaven. Before John describes the church's present and future suffering, he records a vision of God on his throne, worshiped by the angels of heaven (Revelation 4:1-11). The overall purpose of chapter 4 answers the question, "Who is in control of history?" The answer: the Sovereign God, sitting on heaven's throne. Chapter 5 answers the question, "Who will implement God's plan in history?" The answer: a Lion who is also a Lamb. Only he is worthy to take the scroll and remove its seals.

The Seven Seals (Revelation 6:1–8:5)

In this section, John portrays the removal of the seals. The first six seals are removed in Revelation 6:1-17. The first four seals are similar: victory in battle, war and slaughter, famine, and death (Revelation 6:1-8). The fifth (martyrs under the altar crying out for justice) and sixth seals (natural disasters) are quite distinct from the first four (Revelation 6:9-17).

Chapter 7 provides an interlude between the sixth and seventh seal. The chapter answers the question concluding chapter 6, "For the great day of their wrath has come, and who is able to survive?" How will the people of God survive? The answer comes in the form of two visions. The first vision represents 144,000 "servants of our God" about to enter the great tribulation, who have God's seal placed on their forehead (Revelation 7:1-8, KJV). The second vision represents an innumerable multitude of God's people on the other side of the Great Tribulation (Revelation 7:9-17). One wonders what will happen when the seventh seal is broken, considering the devastation of the sixth seal. In Revelation 8:1-5, the seventh seal is removed, which results in silence in heaven. In a very real sense, the seventh seal introduces the seven trumpets.

The Seven Trumpets (Revelation 8:6–11:19)

Next John portrays the disasters on the earth from six trumpet blasts from six angels. The first four trumpet blasts occur in rapid-fire succession and bring devastation upon nature (Revelation 8:6-13). The fifth (locusts from the bottomless pit) and sixth (a massive army from the east) trumpet blasts are described in much greater detail than the first four (Revelation 9:1-21). The images are both horrific and terrifying. Their appalling description suggests they are demonic beings.

In Revelation 10:1–11:14, we have another interlude consisting of two visions. In the first vision, an angel instructs John to eat a little scroll (Revelation 10:1-11). The scroll tastes sweet in his mouth but bitter in his stomach. The sweetness of the scroll indicates the end approaches, while the bitterness of the scroll reveals that God's people must still endure much suffering. The second vision reveals that while God's people are protected spiritually from harm (the measuring of the inner court and the altar), they will suffer physical persecution and martyrdom (the trampling of the outer courts and death of the two witnesses; see Revelation 11:1-14). The seventh trumpet, as the seventh seal, contains no specific devastation, but instead records praises to God for his coming triumph (Revelation 11:15-19).

Behind the Scenes of the Great War (Revelation 12:1–14:20)

In these chapters, John goes behind the scenes of human history. In chapter 12, John answers the question, "Why does Satan hate the church?" The answer: Satan has been defeated at the cross (in heavenly combat) and cast down to earth (Revelation 12:7-12). Satan knows his time is short and goes off to make war against God's people (Revelation 12:13-17). In chapter 13, John answers the question, "How will Satan attempt to destroy God's people in the last days?" The answer: by a beast from the sea (the Antichrist, Revelation 13:1-10) and by a beast from the earth (the false prophet, 13:11-18).

In Revelation 14:1-5, John answers the question, "What will happen to those who refuse the mark of the beast?" The first group consists of 144,000 worshiping the Lamb on Mount Zion; they are still all alive at the end of the Great Tribulation. In Revelation

14:6-20, John answers the question, "What will happen to those who have received the mark of the beast?" We see this second group in three images of judgment: the cup of unmixed wine, the grain harvest, and the winepress.

The Seven Bowls (Revelation 15:1–16:21)

Now John arrives at the seven bowls, the final display of God's judgment. In Revelation 15:1, John describes seven angels holding the seven bowls. Before the angels pour out their bowls, John records the Song of Moses and the Lamb (Revelation 15:3-4) and the Temple in heaven is filled with smoke (Revelation 15:5-8). The seven bowls containing the wrath of God are poured out in rapid-fire succession (Revelation 16:1-21). Unlike the seals and trumpets, no interlude comes between the sixth and seventh bowl. The seventh bowl precedes an earthquake that destroys the great city of Babylon, which represents the world in opposition to God (Revelation 16:19-21).

The Fall of Babylon the Great (Revelation 17:1–19:10)

In this section, John elaborates on the seventh bowl and the fall of Babylon. In chapter 17, he describes Babylon as a harlot. In chapter 18, he describes Babylon as a prosperous and impregnable city, seemingly invincible—but which is destroyed in a brief period. After praise in heaven for Babylon's destruction (Revelation 19:1-5), John describes the marriage supper of the Lamb (Revelation 19:6-10).

Seven Final Events and the Triumph of God (Revelation 19:11–22:5)

John narrates God's triumph in seven final events: (1) the return of Christ (Revelation 19:11-16); (2) the defeat of the Antichrist and his forces at Armageddon (Revelation 19:17-21); (3) Satan's binding (Revelation 20:1-3); (4) Christ's millennial reign (Revelation 20:4-6); (5) Satan's final doom (Revelation 20:7-10); (6) the Great White Throne Judgment (Revelation 20:11-15); and (7) the new heaven, new earth, and new Jerusalem (Revelation 21:1–22:5).

Conclusion (Revelation 22:6-21)

Revelation concludes with a statement concerning the trustworthiness of everything John has seen and heard (Revelation 22:6-15), an invitation for all who are thirsty (Revelation 22:16-17), a warning to any who would add or take away from the prophecy of this book (Revelation 22:18-19), and a benediction including a prayer for Jesus to come quickly (Revelation 22:20-21).

Living Out the Message of Revelation

Revelation has much to teach Christians. First, since God controls history, believers have no reason to fear the future. The one seated on heaven's throne remains in control. God's sovereignty should comfort Christians and not cause them fear, but instead inspire us to trust him.

Second, Revelation emphasizes the person and work of Christ. The book clearly affirms Jesus' deity. The one who died for Christians is their Lord and Savior. Jesus will come again, riding on a white horse. Jesus came the first time to die, but the second time he comes as Judge. The first time Jesus came, most of the world did not even know he had arrived. This time when he comes, every eye will see him. Because Jesus is both Lord and Savior, we should love him more passionately and sing to him more loudly. Because Jesus is coming again, we should feel inspired to more faithfully witness for him.

Finally, Revelation reminds us that we are in a spiritual war, not against flesh and blood (cf. Ephesians 6:12), but against spiritual powers. Revelation takes us behind the scenes of human history to help us better understand this war and what is at stake. Revelation makes perfectly clear, however, that Christ won the war at the cross. These final battles will culminate in Christ's ultimate victory over all his enemies.

Acknowledgments

I WOULD LIKE TO ACKNOWLEDGE several individuals as I complete this book. First, I am extremely grateful to Dr. Thom Rainer for the invitation to write *Journey through the New Testament*. Dr. Rainer is one of the most influential Christian leaders of our day, and I am greatly honored to consider him a friend.

I thank God for the able assistance of Graham Faulkner and Adam Cole in the writing process. Walker Downs remains a blessing to me as he aided me significantly in the editing process. The kind folks at Church Answers demonstrated great patience with me throughout the entire process. I am grateful to my editor, Steve Halliday, and the copyeditors at Tyndale House whose work made this volume much better. Thank you!

Last, but certainly not least, words can never express the depth of my love and appreciation for my wife, Jaylynn. She is truly a gracious gift to me from God.

Notes

1. J. Hampton Keathley III, "The Historical Books of the New Testament," Bible.org, August 4, 2004, https://bible.org/seriespage/3-historical-books -new-testament.
2. For other similar statements, see Matthew 2:5-6; 3:3; 10:34-35; 11:10; 13:14-15; 15:7-9; 21:13, 16, 42; 26:31.
3. The most reliable early manuscripts of the Gospel of Mark end at 16:8. Other manuscripts include various endings to the Gospel.
4. Michael Wilcock, *The Message of Luke: The Saviour of the World* (Downers Grove, IL: InterVarsity Press, 1979), 18.
5. Eugene H. Peterson, introductory note on the book of Acts in *The Message: The New Testament in Contemporary English* (Colorado Springs, CO: NavPress, 1993, 2002, 2018), 1389.
6. See the comments in chapter 3 on Luke's Gospel for what we can know about Luke as a person.
7. The term *epistle* is a more formal way to refer to the New Testament letters. I will use the two terms interchangeably.
8. Eugene H. Peterson, introductory note on the book of 2 Corinthians in *The Message: The New Testament in Contemporary English* (Colorado Springs, CO: NavPress, 1993, 2002, 2018), 1472.
9. For a more complete discussion on the topic of spiritual warfare, see William F. Cook III and Chuck E. Lawless, *Spiritual Warfare in the Storyline of Scripture: A Biblical, Theological, and Practical Approach* (Nashville: B&H Academic, 2019).
10. Dick Lucas, *The Message of Colossians and Philemon*, rev. ed., The Bible Speaks Today, ed. John R. W. Stott (Downers Grove, IL: InterVarsity Press, 2020), 29.
11. On the issue of Pauline authorship, see the comments on 1 Timothy.

12. Michael Green, *The Second Epistle General of Peter, and the General Epistle of Jude: An Introduction and Commentary* (Leicester, England: Inter-Varsity, 1968, 1984), 11.

13. Eugene H. Peterson, introductory note on the books of 1, 2, and 3 John in *The Message: The New Testament in Contemporary English* (Colorado Springs, CO: NavPress, 1993, 2002, 2018), 1561.

14. John R. W. Stott, *The Epistles of John: An Introduction and Commentary*, The Tyndale New Testament Commentaries (Grand Rapids, MI: William B. Eerdmans, 1964), 204–5.

15. For a full discussion, see Cook and Lawless, *Spiritual Warfare in the Storyline of Scripture*.

About the Author

Dr. William F. Cook III is professor of New Testament interpretation at The Southern Baptist Theological Seminary. Before joining the faculty at SBTS, he was associate professor of New Testament and chair of the theology division at Florida Baptist Theological College. He is the author of several books, including a commentary titled *John: Jesus Christ Is God.* Dr. Cook is the coauthor of *Spiritual Warfare in the Storyline of Scripture: A Biblical, Theological, and Practical Approach.* He is also editor of the 40 Days in the Word series and author of the volume on Mark. Since 2001, he has served as lead pastor at the Ninth and O Baptist Church in Louisville.

If you liked this book, you'll want to get involved in

Church Member Equip!

—   —

Do you have a
desire to learn
more about
serving God
through your
local church?

Would you like
to see how
God can use
you in new and
exciting ways?

Get your church
involved in
Church Member
Equip, an
online ministry
designed to
prepare church
leaders and
church members
to better serve
God's mission
and purpose.

Check us out at   **www.ChurchMemberEquip.com**

CHURCH ANSWERS
FEATURING THOM RAINER

CP1749